THE SIGMA MALE BIBLE

BY WILL WILDE

"An investment in knowledge pays the best interest"

- Benjamin Franklin.

GET A FREE AUDIOBOOK

EMAIL SUBJECT LINE:

"SIGMA MALE BIBLE"

TO

MINDSETMASTERSHIP@GMAIL.COM

Want Free New Book Launches?

Email us at:

mindsetmastership@gmail.com

& Follow us on Instagram!
@MindsetMastership

MASTERSHIP BOOKS

UK | USA | Canada | Ireland | Australia
India | New Zealand | South Africa | China

Mastership Books is part of the United Arts Publishing House group of companies based
in London, England, UK.

First published by Mastership Books (London, UK), 2022

I S B N: 978-1-915002-31-0

Cover design by Rich © United Arts Publishing (UK)
Text and internal design by Rich © United Arts Publishing (UK)
Image credits reserved.
Colour separation by Spitting Image Design Studio
Printed and bound in Great Britain

National Publications Association of Britain
London, England, United Kingdom.
Paper design UAP

ISBN: 978-1-915002-31-0 (paperback)

A723.5

Title: Sigma Male Bible

Design, Bound & Printed:

London, England,
Great Britain.

About the Author

Will Wilde

British Male Masculinity, Dating & Behaviour Researcher

Based in London, England.

The Will Wilde team works as a collective; we work with the most senior in men's dating academic research and contemporaries to expand men's thinking & knowledge.

We are in the changing lives business.

Contents

INTRODUCTION

Meaning of Sigma Male

Once upon a time, males were described as either the Alpha Male or the Beta Male. With their leadership characteristics, self-assurance, and no-nonsense outlook on life, Alpha Males led the pack. The alternative consisted of submissive and compliant beta males. However, the more we understand people, the more we realize that there are variants of Alpha and Beta, and a new personality type appears to be emerging, the sigma male. Sigma Male describes an individual who is neither Alpha nor Beta and follows his rhythm. The Sigma Male is now a trending topic in modern psychology, and people are paying close attention to what this new personality type is doing in the world. Sigma Males have always existed, doing their own thing on the social margins. These individuals are rule breakers and creators. They garner a lot of Attention for both positive and negative reasons, but it's what we don't know about these personality types that keeps people interested. A Sigma Male is a man who prefers to live outside of the traditional social dominance hierarchy. Sigma males have characteristics of alpha males, but they prefer to walk to the beat of their drum, rarely accept commands from others, and refuse to comply with society's labels and classifications.

They are not dependent on society in the same manner as other guys. They are often nomadic, self-employed individuals who value education and experience over material belongings and employment. Sigma Males were formerly considered an uncommon type of guy, but with the growth of the internet and the freedom to work and live anywhere, Sigma Males are now emerging from the shadows, out of their shells and becoming more common. They appear to be appealing to women because of their independent nature and capability of meeting personal requirements without relying on anybody or anything else. Sigma Males are not as far away from society's hierarchy as they would have you think. Many are unaware of their vital position in traditional hierarchical civilizations worldwide. Sigma Males typically venture beyond their comfort zones, produce great works of art, launch enterprises, are confident and quiet partners, and are diligent employees. Some may believe that Sigma Males withdraw from society because of laziness or unwillingness to work, although the contrary is true. They require time and space to construct their ideas and realize their ambitions. Whether or not they know it, their purpose is to prepare the way for many others, even Alpha Males, who aren't as innovative or ready to go against the grain to allow civilization to advance. People adore but do not entirely comprehend this segment of society.

Characteristics of A Sigma Male

Here are a few characteristics of a man who fits the category of Sigma.

They Are Recluse

It should not be confused with Sigma males disliking social interaction. Instead, it indicates that individuals rarely depend on others for enjoyment, and conversely, they may be friendly and cordial towards those they like.

They Are Flexible

While Alpha and Beta guys are more set in their personalities and preferred locations, Sigma males may adjust to nearly any situation. They can function effectively in various social circumstances, team configurations, and even outside their comfort zones. Regardless of who is observing, they are themselves. Sigma males prefer to be themselves irrespective of who is there, while others may be more friendly or present a particular image to the public. Surprisingly, they are essentially the same person when alone as with other people.

They May Lead Without Using Power

When we consider leaders, we typically envision Alpha males. Sigma males also make outstanding leaders, but with a unique leadership style. They favor leading by example or mutual dialogue over asserting their control or authority. With a well-balanced approach to leadership, Sigmas will achieve their objectives.

They Are Attentive Listeners

As a matter of reciprocal civility, Sigma males tend to be attentive listeners because they recognize the need for quiet and respect when others are speaking. They place greater emphasis on the substance than the volume, so they listen carefully and speak only when necessary.

They Are Self-Conscious

This may be true for Beta guys, but it frequently manifests in their insecurity. When we say that Sigma males are self-conscious, they know their strengths and weaknesses. Self-awareness enables people to self-correct when they make a mistake, preventing them from repeating errors.

They Possess a Murky Morality

In difficult situations, Sigma males tend to see right and wrong. As a result, they may retain a compassionate view toward particular individuals rather than condemning them categorically. In addition, they develop the ability to assess all facets of a problem before rendering a verdict.

Their Social Skills Are Rusty

Sigma males might appear brusque or indifferent due to their lack of emotional responses and straight communication style. This is a byproduct of their excellent listening skills, which others may perceive as impolite. They do not conceal their intentions by flowery rhetoric or flattery. They can fit into buddy groups but do not rely on them. Sigma males are adaptable, making it simple to join many social groups and get along with others. However, this does not imply that they rely on social groups or friends, and they remain the same regardless

They Choose Their Fate

While Alphas flourish in a high-functioning atmosphere and Betas do well in a low-stress, passive one, Sigma males succeed or fail on their terms. They recognize that they are accountable for their destinies, are less reliant on society and surroundings, and hold themselves responsible for their activities and results.

Their Social Networks are often Small Yet Tight

Sigma males have little desire to have large buddy groups or impress large crowds, and they would rather have a smaller group of close friends with whom they can trust and share the same worldview. Although it may appear antisocial, it is not.

They Are Self-Reliant

Sigma males prioritize independence above all else and want to be entirely self-reliant in all realms of life. They do not wish to rely on others for life's necessities; thus, they develop the skills necessary to live independently.

They Take Chances Without Fear

Sigmas may often depart from established professions and life paths and rarely stick to a particular decision. They reject societal systems and shackles and want to do their own thing. Additionally, they acknowledge the inherent risks with their decision.

They Are Not Seeking Attention

Sigma males do not want external affirmation or attention and do not seek it out or thrive on it when they obtain it. Instead of becoming the focus of attention, they like to blend into the background and listen and observe.

They Can Become an Alpha

A Sigma male might be an Alpha male due to his social adaptability and versatility. Sigma males' independence and leadership qualities play to their strengths and comfort zones.

Expectations Are Irrelevant to Them

It's often thought Alphas are at the top, and betas are followers; however, sigmas just don't fit the model. Sigmas have little interest in the hierarchy and disregard all societal conventions and trends (especially those imposed by alphas). You cannot dictate how they dress or behave, acting autonomously.

They Are Rule-Breakers

Identical to alpha men, sigma males battle with authority. Sigmas are often self-employed and place a premium on peace and adaptability. They are better off working independently because they have no problem managing their time and being organized.

They Do Not Seek Approval

To feel fulfilled and successful, Sigma males do not rely on luxury. They do not attempt to legitimize themselves with expensive items because they realize that material possessions cannot replace self-worth. So they drive any car they want, dress however they want, and do not follow alphas' directives. Their motto is "Be yourself."

They Are Not Approachable to Everybody

Sigmas do not brag on social media about their accomplishments or ambitions. Private are their interests, and people frequently view them as coy and secretive. Understanding sigmas requires some time, and they feel no need to disclose their personal information. They want ego boosts and affirmation as much as fish require bicycles.

They Stay Modest as Leaders

Sigma males are lone wolves; nevertheless, they may become imposing leaders under the right conditions. Their enthusiasm and commitment inspire others. Sigmas in prominent positions are not arrogant, so they are admired.

Individualism is Their Priority

Sigma males are particular about their habits, and a dominating individual is their worst enemy. They disregard the expectations of others, and Sigmas only alter if they desire it.

They Are Confident Introverts

Sigmas like being alone and dislike being the center of attention. Sigmas have the same self-assurance as alphas, even though they are frequently unnoticed. Extraversion is the only defining characteristic of alphas.

Personal Space is a Necessity

Sigma males require a lot of personal space to achieve their learning and success goals. They can make drastic changes to pursue their passion, such as disappearing. Nobody can stand in the way of a Sigma.

Sigma Male Zodiac Signs

There is no single zodiac sign exclusively associated with Sigma Males. Nonetheless, a few zodiac signs have similar characteristics to Sigma's to define its behavior. The typical self-assured and sociable male is not a Scorpio. Yes, they are confident but mysterious and not particularly impressed by authority. This does not imply that they are bad boys; instead, they are content with their choices.

Capricorns — are confident loners. They recognize their intelligence but will not flaunt it. They are kind and willing to assist even if they do not remember what they do. Leos and Sagittarians may also possess confidence but lean more towards being Alphas. Again, there are no restrictions on what Zodiac Sign one must have to be a Sigma. The two terms listed above are the closest matches if we must adhere to strict descriptions.

Sigma Male Symbols (The lone wolf)

It is common to compare the Sigma Male to a lone wolf. He is fierce and mysterious despite living alone and apart from the pack. The Sigma possesses sufficient strength to defend himself and attack if necessary. In contrast to the Alpha, he does not require a pack to follow him around to feel confident.

Benefits of The Sigma Male Lifestyle

Sigma males choose to follow their path rather than that of another. They pursue their interests, and this way of life is liberating without obligations to other people or circumstances. Being a sigma male does not entail the responsibilities of being an alpha.

- They are not hindered by their family, tribe, residence, or commitments and are not required to consider other individuals when making decisions.

- They Have Clarity of Mind: Sigma males know what they want and pursue. Since their goals and desires are unaffected by the actions of others, they exert maximum effort to attain them.

- They avoid people and drama, as they do not wish to inadvertently carry the emotional baggage of others. Therefore, it could be said they avoid forming too many interpersonal relationships.

- Sigmas possess qualities that women generally find attractive. They state their expectations for the relationship and do not make false promises. They are self-assured, attractive, and mysterious without being possessive or needy.

Drawbacks of The Sigma Male Lifestyle

Sigmas are introverted men who dislike mixing with others and forming strong bonds with a large number of individuals. The majority of people believe that they are lonely, but sigmas disagree.

They Are Commitment-Averse: Most sigma males avoid committed relationships because they do not want to commit. Committing to someone entails responsibilities and being a member of a group of friends and family, which contradicts Sigma's introverted and solitary nature. In addition, Sigmas may appear emotionally distant.

Key Takeaways

- A Sigma Male is a man who prefers to live outside of the traditional social dominance hierarchy.

- Sigma males have characteristics of alpha males, but they prefer to walk to the beat of their drum, rarely accept commands from others, and refuse to comply with society's labels and classifications.

- Sigma males prioritize independence above all things and want to be entirely self-reliant in all realms of life.

- Sigma males require a lot of personal space to achieve their learning and success goals.

- It is common to compare the Sigma Male to a lone wolf. He is fierce and mysterious despite living alone and apart from the pack.

CHAPTER 1

SIGMA MALE ROMANCE AND RELATIONSHIP

Sigma Males in Love and Friendship

Even though Sigma Male is a loner, he does not intend to remain alone forever. He is naturally independent and may not actively seek companionship, but he welcomes the opportunity when it presents itself. He approaches affection and friendship on his terms.

Do Sigma Males Fall in Love?

A Sigma is a man with healthy desires. He can certainly fall in love. Sigma Males are the same as Alpha Males in the Socio-sexual Hierarchy, which must be understood. However, he has placed himself outside of the structure on purpose. Some women find him even more attractive since he exudes confidence without overtly utilizing his charms. Indeed, the Sigma Male can fall in love. Also, he desires women and takes them so seriously that he is not playing games.

A Sigma holds more traditional notions about love. However, notice that he will not actively pursue love and passion and allows things to come to him.

Do Sigma Males Have Friends?

A Sigma Male might have a few friends. However, he views it as a choice and not a need.

Unique Signs That a Woman Sees You as a Sigma Male

Typically, when people hear Sigma Male, they usually pigeonhole this personality as a low value outsider; perhaps a substance abuser, criminal, male chauvinist, etc. However, this is an entirely false perception of the sigma males. In reality, sigma males are neither random drug users nor criminals, and they exemplify males with an original perspective, innovative thought, and elusive conduct. We refer to them as the progress of humanity since their vision is vastly distinct from that of the typical man. The cognitive pattern of sigma males directly contradicts what most men are raised to believe. Most sigma males' characteristics and behavioral patterns stem from their life experiences. You cannot learn them in school, and your parents will not teach them to you. However, there is something that few men know. Most women perceive mainly three categories of men: Alpha, Beta, and Sigma. Regrettably, more alpha and beta males dominate the globe nowadays. These males conform to society's fictitious dominance order.

Women are often accustomed to dealing with Alpha and Beta males. Do you realize why? Because genuine sigma males are few in the world. Consequently, they have distinctive thinking, behavior style, and worldview. Other men, however, have become sigma males over time by consistent practice and the deliberate adoption of particular behavioral features.

But here's the thing: a woman can tell within the first few seconds of conversation if you are a sigma, Alpha, or beta male. And how this woman will treat you will depend on the personality type she believes you to be.

When You Are Self-Reliant

When a woman appears independent in your presence, she may view you as a sigma male. Everyone knows that sigma males value their independence and prefer to date women who love their autonomy. Therefore, if a woman believes you to be a sigma male, she will strive to be as independent as possible when you are present. She will demonstrate independence through her body language, voice tone, and response during a conversation.

She Provides Sufficient Space

Once a woman recognizes specific characteristics of a sigma male in you, she will begin to give you space. These women are aware that regardless of how much a sigma male loves a person, once that individual starts to suffocate them with their presence, the lone wolves lose interest rapidly. Therefore, if a woman believes you to be a sigma male, she will give you adequate space. They are aware that solitude leads to happiness. Consequently, they allow you to spend time alone and contemplate the world naturally.

She Speaks as Little as Possible

A woman who speaks excessively irritates Sigma males. Furthermore, these women are aware of this fact. Therefore, if they believe you to be a sigma male, they will attempt to say as little as possible. Even when they want to have a conversation with you, they try to prioritize thinking over speaking. Because these women do not want to appear unintelligent and foolish in front of you, they will attempt to analyze their words before speaking. Once you observe that a woman is attentive to what she says around you, she believes you are a sigma male.

Submission

When in the presence of a sigma male, women always act submissively. Once a woman identifies you as a sigma male, she will look at you with wide eyes and position her body to attract your attention. In reality, sigma males are too bright and intelligent for most women to handle.

So, once they realize they cannot compete with the sigma males' intelligence and perception, they will unconsciously become submissive. In reality, however, sigma males prefer to date women who are self-reliant and have a unique worldview; women who can engage in an intellectual conversation with lone wolves and are willing to take risks for self-progression. Once a woman possesses these characteristics, she will be attractive to sigma males.

She Pursues You

Most women will recognize you as a sigma male if you are a masculine man of high value with a distinctive mindset. Because genuine sigma males are so rare, they will continuously pursue you. They will want to experience the mystique and evasion of the sigma male. Girls instinctively regard every lone wolf as a man of exceptional worth. Many women find sigma males irresistible and desire to be with them. The same cannot be said about the beta male, however. These men pursue women constantly. And the more a beta male pursues a woman, the further away she moves from him.

Sigma Male Traits That Drive Women Crazy

Here are characteristics of Sigma males that drive women crazy;

Leadership

A Sigma Male possesses all leadership qualities. In other words, they are leaders by nature. However, they prefer to work alone. Even if they become leaders in the future, they lead by example. They do not issue orders from the convenience of their office, and they are constantly at the forefront of implementing strategies to assist their team in accomplishing its objectives. The Sigma Males dislike being in charge for so long. Because they despise being conditioned to a specific social framework. And the fact that Sigma males do not enjoy proving a point or creating unnecessary drama makes them quite attractive, and a Sigma Male is what most ladies crave.

Mysterious

Everything with sigma males is mysterious. They desire neither conformity nor distinction and understand how to conduct themselves with females. Being mysterious is one of the characteristics of Sigma Male that drives women wild.

Observer

Every Sigma Male is an intelligent observer. And his capacity to observe enables him to make better-informed assessments of people and circumstances consistently. Sigma Male is not perfect, and he sometimes makes errors. But when he does, he immediately gains insight from them. This is why Sigma Male seldom makes the same error twice.

Dominant Introvert

This is one of Sigma Male's unique qualities that makes them appealing to women. The Sigma Male is an introverted dominant male that dislikes attracting unwarranted attention to himself. Therefore, he rarely speaks or contributes at meetings or social events and loves listening and seeing others talk. A Sigma Male would instead devote his energies to contemplation and introspection rather than useless contact, which is one factor that provides him with a strategic edge.

Extremely Adaptable

One of the characteristics of Sigma Male that drives women insane is his adaptability. You cannot ever surprise a Sigma Male. Occasionally, the Sigma Male's adaptation is so natural that they may appear to have successfully integrated into the hierarchy.

Charismatic

Even though he would not want to show it, the Sigma Male is exceptionally charming. He can get along with persons of various personalities. Again, Sigma Males are attractive. And his drive, charisma, and inner appeal assist them in attaining their business goals.

Freedom Lover

Generally, Sigma Males are unable to perform well in social structures. They cherish their independence and freedom more than anything else imaginable. Therefore, they appreciate the luxury of their own company. In addition, they perceive others around them as energy-sucking vampires.

Solo Artist

Sigma Males do not play well with others. They can adjust to any circumstance, but they prefer to operate independently. Therefore, they are commonly referred to as the lone wolf. He enjoys establishing his ideals and forging his way. Typically, Sigma Males construct their games and sets of rules. However, he cooperates with others when it is required. And once they find others who share their objectives, Sigma Male can reach significant commercial and relationship milestones.

Rebel

Sigma Males are the most defiant of all-male personality types, and they are rule-breakers and norm-defiers, which is one reason why Sigma Males find women attractive. Generally speaking, Sigma Males dislike conformity because they have other options. But because they have the opportunity to, they are using this liberty. Unlike other male types, Sigma Male wields authority by violating the norms.

Independent

One of the reasons why Sigma Male is appealing to women is his independence, and Sigma Males rely on no other individuals for anything. The Sigma Male cares about his close friends, family, and lovers. However, they want people to be a supplementary aspect of their life, not the central emphasis. The affirmation of others does not drive them. One of the reasons Sigma Males are so exceptional is that their inspiration originates from inside.

Respectful

Despite his singularity, the Sigma Male is highly courteous. While he desires his independence, he respects the freedom of others above all else. Because Sigma Males cherish the liberty of others, they seldom impose rules or restrictions on others. Even if individuals do not behave as he desires, a Sigma Male makes no effort to manipulate or convince them. Instead, he will pursue his course. And this is because Sigma Males respect others naturally.

Personal Space Enthusiast

Every Sigma Male values their privacy. Even when in a relationship, they enjoy establishing limits. They are very protective of their personal space and will not tolerate intrusions. However, Sigma males will gladly share their personal space with close friends, partners, and family members with whom they share a special bond.

Craziest Things Only the Sigma Males Know About Women

Most people view sigma males as oddballs who are unhappy with their lives, and these individuals never accept the notion of sigma masculinity. Possibly because they are feeble, worthless men with little self-respect. Consequently, they expect every other man to be on par with them. Every high-value sigma male comprehends the female psyche. They understand the motivations behind women's behavior and can easily forecast their best moves. One of the reasons women find sigma males so attractive is that they constantly look elusive and enigmatic.

Women Are Programmed to Evaluate Men

Since the beginning of time, women have always evaluated male suitors based on their power, maturity, and masculinity. They're unlikely to stop anytime soon because it is a part of the choosing when filtering potential partners, and it seems to be unchanging anytime soon. Most men (particularly Alpha males) are not prepared to hear this. However, women are naturally attracted to the finest males imaginable. They desire an emotionally robust, mature man with a distinct outlook on life. The most meticulous and detail-oriented ladies always assess a man's strength. Interestingly, such is the subtle assessments most men don't realize it's a test.

She will complete the task in the most natural manner imaginable. A lady may test your emotional strength during a conversation and how you respond to difficulties. It's amusing that several men wish women wouldn't just test them. Perhaps it is because they lack the average male's confidence and mental strength. There is no question about that. Before entering a committed relationship, most women will evaluate your mental strength and masculinity. Expecting a sigma or high-value woman to have a relationship with you without testing is like requesting that the sun not rise. Women are constantly attracted to men with strong personalities and distinct characteristics, such as the sigma males. Sigma males are the sort of men that women want. When in the presence of a woman, these characteristics appear unintentionally, making the lone wolf the ideal gentleman. Again, sigma males know that testing men are part of women's biological process. Therefore, they do not take these examinations themselves. They accept it as part of their identity and make no fuss about it.

Women Can Identify Beta Males

Women have genetic advantages that enable them to identify low-status males, such as Beta and Omega males. Even if these men falsify their personalities and present themselves as sigma males, women of high value will still recognize them. Remember that to a choosing female, a low-value male will always be a man of low worth, regardless of how he attempts to disguise himself. Sigma males feel it is hard to mislead a woman by pretending to be someone else. Even if the woman first trusts you, she will soon discover the truth. So many phony sigma males exist, and they assume the role and continue to act accordingly. But as we all know, the sun, the moon, and the truth cannot remain hidden for long. Therefore, the truth will eventually emerge regardless of how you attempt to conceal your true personality.

Less is More

Most men are unaware of this fact, which is why women gravitate towards sigma males. They understand the psychology of women and are aware that the less attention a woman receives, the more intrigued she becomes. Yes, we know that ladies require care, but they will lose interest in you when you offer them excessive attention. Indeed, that is somewhat contradictory, yet that is the fact. Have you ever observed that your ex-girlfriend becomes more interested in you following a breakup? Because the less attention you pay to her, the more appealing you become. Sigma males are always the dominating partner in a relationship because they pay less attention to women and come across as secretive. I do not believe this to be attention-grabbing. You may have the opposite effect when you give a woman costly presents or take her on a luxurious vacation. The less attention and presents you offer a lady, the more attention she will give you. Remember that women's greatest dreams include things that they cannot get. Therefore, you become her greatest dream if she cannot have your undivided attention. Once you realize that little is more with women, you will have a new viewpoint on them.

Sigma males are aware of these realities, making them the most desirable male personality in the manosphere.

What Girls Think About Most Sigma Males

The sigma male is every woman's fantasy, and they are what 99.9 percent of women would characterize as the ideal partner. Everything about the sigma males is outstanding, from their outlook on life to their unflinching concentration and composure. Even the most independent and obstinate woman will naturally submit to sigma males. His aura inspires reverence, and his original ideas and theories are superior. The sigma male may not have the ideal appearance and may not possess the perfect physique. But after conversing with him and working with him for a few hours, you will realize that lone wolf are perfection incarnate. I mean, they have the most incredible personality in history. Without question, the sigma male is a unique individual. The majority of women are consistently intimidated by sigma males. Why do women feel intimidated anytime they are in the presence of a sigma male?

She Avoids Making Eye Contact

Avoiding eye contact with you is one of the indicators that a woman may be intimidated by you. When a woman avoids eye contact, she establishes a protective barrier in her mind. However, here is what you need to know. When a woman is intimidated by you, she will avoid making eye contact. You may see that she is sometimes stealing looks toward you when you gaze in her way. However, she will avert eye contact when she meets your gaze. Moreover, if you observe her, you can notice the timidity in her expression.

This timidity shows that she likes you but wishes to conceal it. You should consider this if you believe she is the lady you want to be with.

Her Body Language

The easiest way for sigma males to understand the minds of others is by their body language. You may readily determine whether a lady is frightened by you by observing her body language. For example, if a lady directs her entire body toward you, it implies that she is not scared by you, demonstrating that she is pleased to meet you. However, when a female is scared by you, she will turn her body slightly to the right or left when speaking with you. How a woman places her body may be a protective mechanism caused by her fear of you. In contrast, women are typically drawn to males they fear or males that other men dread. Girls turn their bodies slightly while conversing with men they are uncomfortable with, so they may leave the discussion without embarrassment.

She Speaks in a Lower Tone

When intimidated by you, women tend to talk in a lower and gentler tone. Perhaps it is because they find you enigmatic and challenging to comprehend your nature. Every sigma male must have encountered this in some capacity. A female may be noisy with her friends but becomes abruptly silent as you approach. And when she speaks, she does it with a calm and quiet voice.

She Gets Uncomfortable in Your Presence

There are several things that women do when scared by their personality. They may fidget with their hair (known as hair flipping) or act to make it clear she is uncomfortable with you.

She Pauses Before and After Her Statements

One of the signals that a lady is frightened by you is an awkward silence during a discussion. A woman's defensive mechanism causes her to pause during a discussion. Therefore, if you observe a lady pausing when conversing with you, she is scared of you. In conclusion, most women feel naturally terrified by males they have recently met or do not know well. Perhaps this is because men are typically physically stronger than women. In addition, certain males are capable to commit unspeakable atrocities against women. Therefore, it is common for intelligent women to seem intimidated or avoid men they do not know well. However, when a woman timidly exhibits the indicators outlined in this section, it is clear that she considers you beautiful.

The Mystery of Women's Attraction to Sigma Male

Most women are attracted to mysterious men, giving sigma males an advantage. They believe they can convince a sigma male to commit and are frequently drawn to them.

Sigma males do not need to commit to a relationship entirely, and they may terminate it at any time. Most sigmas are completely forthright with women regarding their desires, which comes across as self-assurance to most women, a trait women admire. Sigma males are attractive, mysterious, and solitary. They are challenging to restrain and rebellious because they follow their path. However, sigma males rarely commit to a single woman because of the burden of companionship. Most Sigma males are not interested in forming a significant emotional relationship with their spouses and want to have fun. Since they have similar personalities and goals, a sigma male and a female may be the most compatible. You will recognize a sigma male if he is an introvert, and yet somewhat dominant, influential, and successful. It is optimistic that they can lead and have a clear mind, but they may not feel comfortable making commitments. It is their charisma that often attracts women to them.

Additionally, it cannot be denied that they can be charming. Although this male is generally a loner, they can be pretty intriguing.

Behaviors Sigma Males Dislike Most About Women

Sigma males are exceptional men who cherish solitude forever. They are lone wolves who always do things their way and march to the beat of their drums. But regardless of their characteristics, sigma males are still human. They have needs and emotions to communicate, and only they possess exceptional emotional intelligence and self-control. A sigma male in a relationship is a mystery. You cannot anticipate his actions or what he will do in the next instant. But one thing is sure: Sigma males adore dating self-sufficient, high-value women. Women who are bright, intelligent, independent, and of great worth are always attractive to lone wolves. And once a sigma male encounters a woman with these characteristics, he is likely to marry her. However, here are some behaviors of women that sigma males dislike the most. Whether a sigma male highly appreciates a woman, the relationship will change if he observes these behaviors.

Let's analyze the five things that sigma males despise most about women. If a sigma observes any of these characteristics in a woman, the relationship may be in jeopardy.

Dishonesty

Sigma males dislike interacting with dishonest individuals. Whether you are their lover, acquaintance, or family member, he will distance himself from you if he discovers your dishonesty. Dating an untrustworthy spouse can be emotionally exhausting for sigma males. Sigma males may despise women with poor self-esteem, codependence, or jealousy, but a sigma male cannot remove dishonesty from the woman he loves. Once a woman has lied to a sigma male, he feels betrayed. And at that point, no amount of apologies can rectify the situation. A dishonest woman can never earn the confidence and respect of a sigma male. Regardless of the circumstances, the sigma male always desires his partner to speak the truth. He would rather be hurt by the truth than soothed by a falsehood.

Nevertheless, why would you lie to a person as sensitive as the sigma male? If you tell the truth, Sigma males will never condemn or make you feel awful about yourself. However, attempting to make people feel good with falsehoods is something they cannot tolerate.

Bringing Up Old Issues

Sigma males are so sensitive to the feelings of others. And he wants the lady he is dating to respect his sentiments. No relationship is perfect, not even the one with a lone wolf. There will always be topics to discuss. The sigma male may inadvertently harm his partner and make her feel awful. And after he acknowledges his errors, a sigma male apologizes swiftly and resolves the situation with you. Sigma males always note what makes their partners furious and ensure it never occurs again. However, a sigma male cannot tolerate his partner bringing up past concerns whenever they quarrel. For the sigma male, it's emotionally taxing. A sigma male wants his ladies to forget and forgive previously discussed difficulties.

However, he finds it unpleasant when a woman repeatedly brings up previous difficulties as revenge. If this continues for a time, sigma males may end their relationship with the woman in private. The last behavior a sigma male desires is a relationship with a woman who is poisonous and emotionally manipulating.

Flirting with All Men

This is a major warning sign for the sigma males. The Lone wolf desires an exclusive connection and will not find it amusing if his wife flirts with every Tom, Dick, and Harry. Do not misunderstand - sigma males are not insecure regarding their ladies. However, they find it abhorrent when their partner flirts with every male they encounter. Sigma males cannot date a woman who disregards their emotions. Once a woman manipulates a sigma male's emotions, he promptly terminates the relationship, regardless of how attractive, sophisticated, or intelligent she may be. Sigma males dislike anything that leaves them feeling emotionally depleted. They would rather be alone than date a lady who manipulates their emotions. How women think is clearly understood by lone wolves. They know that flirting with other males is risky and might lead to infidelity in their relationship. Therefore, he would choose to abandon a relationship that may leave him brokenhearted. Ultimately, lone wolves are more inclined to tackle emotional difficulties objectively.

Not Giving Them Their Own Space

Males of the sigma species are distinguished by their insatiable craving for isolation. This is how they reflect on the surrounding world and replenish their creative energy. No matter how much a sigma male loves a woman, he finds her highly annoying once she becomes excessively possessive. When a sigma male is in a relationship, he does not attempt to dominate or consume his partner's leisure time. He permits them to enjoy a life of freedom and independence. However, the sigma male wants his spouse to treat him similarly. If you attempt to dominate the Lone wolf's life or occupy his spare time, he will view you as a burden. And if he begins to consider you a burden, the relationship may never be the same. Sigma males are a phenomenon in the manosphere because they do not live to impress anybody, not even women. They make their judgments, and if their partner doesn't offer them the freedom to pursue other interests, they may reassess the relationship. Once a sigma male decides to review a relationship, the outcome is not always positive.

Excessive Drama

Dramatic women irritate and are poisonous to Sigma males. Men may find the theatrical conduct of women exciting and amusing. However, acting-up is unpleasant to the lone wolf. Acting like a child to Attract the attention of a sigma male is a massive turnoff. Some behaviors that might cause a sigma male to quit a relationship include nagging, whining, and refusing to admit when they are wrong.

How Sigma Males Spot a Promiscuous Woman

Sigma males place a great deal of importance on a woman's loyalty. The lone wolf seldom enters into relationships, but they demand complete loyalty from their partners. The sigma males may withstand sexual promiscuity. They are not possessive but want their partner to be devoted and faithful. The capacity of sigma males to identify a promiscuous woman gives them an edge and protects them from wasting their time and energy on an unworthy lady. Regrettably, many males are naive in the murky realm of intimate relationships. They invest their time, effort, and resources on women, only to be cheated on by a random male these ladies have never met. A lady who often sleeps with many males is never a wise investment. Although the culture of modern civilization may like to prove differently; however, sigma males feel that prior sexual experience might negatively impact future relationships.

You could consider this book to be judgmental. However, sigma males always prioritize their interests. To defend their interests, lone wolves evaluate the personalities of their closest companions. From her lifestyle to having too many male friends, sigma males utilize the following red signs to identify a promiscuous woman.

Women Who Enjoy Partying Way Too Much

Women who party too much often prefer going out than to have a peaceful night at home. They constantly seek excitement and enjoyment. Once a sigma male observes this attitude in a woman, he knows she is sexually active. First impressions of these ladies may be that they are amusing and intriguing. However, the fact is that their lifestyle ages them quicker. Once they decide to form a relationship, sigma males seek stability. And they cannot obtain it from a lady with a pleasure addiction. Any lady who is unable to remain at home at night needs excitement. Unfortunately, her desire will bite you if you choose to date this lady. When the sigma male decides to settle down, he likes to be with a calm and imaginative woman who would instead read, watch television, and meditate than attend a party.

Women with an Excessive Number of Male Friends

To a sigma male, women with an excessive number of male friends are often promiscuous. Do not misunderstand; there is nothing wrong with a lady conversing with a man. Sigma males will not make a big issue about it, and their women are free to speak with anyone they like. However, they cannot handle having a large number of male pals. When their ladies have close ties with other males and discuss personal matters, the sigma male finds it insulting and annoying. These partnerships might result in split allegiance on the woman's part. Therefore, women with so many male pals are terrible news, and sigma males tend to avoid them.

Women Who Despise Men

Women who often despise men are incapable of loyalty in any relationship. They continually examine males to determine if they are manly enough. They are never content with a single male, no matter how well you treat them. They will be heard making a variety of disparaging remarks against males. They will assert that all men are blah blah blah, that males only care about blah blah blah, etc. I am aware that some men are dreadful in terms of relationships. But if every male a woman encounters is awful, shouldn't we examine the common denominator more closely? Sigma males feel that women constantly moan about the men in their lives are either still resentful about a broken relationship or portray themselves as objects of attraction.

Women Who Are Social Media Addicts

The sigma males feel that social media addicts are likely to engage in sexual activity. These ladies love drama and attention, have numerous male internet acquaintances, and are always online conversing with each Tom, Dick, and Harry. These ladies assume that their attractiveness is directly linked to the number of friends and likes they receive. Once a sigma male discovers that a woman is so attached to her phone and addicted to social media that she pays her partner little or no attention, it is clear that she is promiscuous.

She is Interested in Promiscuous Celebrity Figures

Sigma males are always cautious towards women who are interested in promiscuous celebrities. These women are prone to promiscuity since they do not consider having several male partners a significant issue. Therefore, once a Sigma male studies a woman and realizes that her friends and role models are promiscuous, he understands she is prone to promiscuity.

Key Takeaways

- A Sigma Male might have a few friends. However, he sees it as a choice and not a need.

- Most women will recognize you as a sigma male if you are a masculine man of high value with a distinctive mindset.

- Everything with sigma males is mysterious. They desire neither conformity nor distinction and understand how to conduct themselves with females.

- The less attention and presents you offer a lady, the more attention she will give you. Therefore, you become her greatest dream if she cannot have your undivided attention.

- Avoiding eye contact with you is one of the indicators that a woman may be intimidated by you.

- Sigma males do not need to commit to a relationship completely, and they may terminate it at any time. Most sigmas are completely forthright with women regarding their desires, which comes across as confidence to most women, a trait women admire.

- Sigma males dislike interacting with dishonest individuals. Whether you are their lover, acquaintance, or family member, he will distance himself from you if he discovers your dishonesty.

- Sigma males place a great deal of importance on a woman's loyalty. The lone wolf seldom enters into relationships, but they demand complete loyalty from their partners.

CHAPTER 2

SIGMA MALE RULE LIST

How Sigma Males Dominate

The Sigma males have the reputation of being lone wolves who exist outside of the imagined social hierarchy. He enjoys his own company and dances to his drumbeats. Lone wolves may not love leading as much as Alpha males; however, their acts and demeanor constantly enable them to control others. Even while working under an Alpha male employer, the lone wolf indirectly controls the alpha male with his brilliant ideas and thoughts.

Sigmas will always oppose established customs and embrace an alternative strategy. Consequently, they are frequently referred to as rule-breakers. This personality type never pursues dominance conventionally; instead, it adds value to the individual and becomes the focus of dominance. Although it is easy to identify a sigma male, it is impossible to determine what motivates them. In other words, their whole identity is predicated on their reluctance to comply with established standards placed on those who wish to ascend the social hierarchy. Interestingly, the Sigma male is more concerned with completing goals that benefit everyone than gaining power. Typically, sigma males avoid fighting whenever feasible.

But when they are in command, they are unafraid of disagreement. However, the leadership style of sigma males differs from that of Alpha male, who attempts to make everyone feel inferior to him. Sigma males avoid confrontation at all costs and never engage in the dominance game with their employees, despite knowing how. This personality type would prefer to let others underestimate them since they have no desire to be noticed.

Sigma Males Enjoy Being Alone

The sigmas' default behavior is to spend time alone. Nonetheless, they may be in the company of other sigmas. People believe sigma males are not intelligent because they can simply blend into the background and go unnoticed. And they frequently undervalue them. Sigma males have a higher IQ than Alpha males and can readily assess circumstances and develop practical solutions unknown to most people. From the outside, sigma males may appear to be weaker males. However, if you take the time to comprehend them, you will discover that they are even more potent than those who seek fame and notoriety. Sigma males are self-assured in their abilities and never seek power and dominance over others. In addition, their inner strength enables people to select meaningful objectives and work toward their attainment. Sigma males are dominant because they can avoid conflict and maintain silence. They thoroughly comprehend the wants and requirements of others, and this enables them to employ their manipulative skills in a very subtle manner.

Sigma males may not like influencing others, but they know their subtle persuasive techniques may carry them far. Sigma males cannot command others to do anything; they may even retreat after offering a proposal. This will show that whatever you do for the sigma male is your idea. This allows the sigma males to attain their goals without forcing their will on others. It is amusing that in a society where the alpha male appears to be the dominant gender, the sigma male truly reigns supreme. They are not as flashy or intriguing as the dominant males. However, they can obtain what they desire. Because sigma males spend more time alone, they have an exceptional capacity to read people and passively persuade them to behave how they choose.

People may not recognize the sigma males for who they are, given that they are always in the shadows. However, if you look closely, you will notice that they make the best of any circumstance without claiming credit. One advantage of sigma males is that they do not exercise authority like alpha males. They will only utilize their dominating nature in response to an opponent's attempt to dominate them. When you attempt to control a sigma male in a certain situation, he will subtly use his skills to outwit you and get the spotlight. Sigma males will obtain anything they desire without detection. This explains why people frequently marvel at the sigma male's ability to remain unnoticed.

Sigma Male Dominance via Non-Dominance

The reality is that the sigma male dominates by not dominating. They conceal their genuine identity on purpose so that others will underestimate them. However, they are more intelligent than they look, and unlike Alpha males, they do not control others. The awareness of human nature possessed by sigma males enables them

.nything they desire from others without being

mination of Sigma males is misinterpreted as weakness. However, this makes them more influential and powerful than those who desire fame and notoriety. You cannot recognize a sigma male based on his appearance or behavior. This is because the key to comprehending the strength of this mystery individual lies inside himself and not outside. The sigma male will never reveal how he obtained what he desired. However, he will create the appearance that it was your idea. Interestingly, sigma males have little interest in popularity or recognition, and they like to remain in the background and rely on others to help them achieve their objectives. The sigma male knows how to harness his abilities to achieve his goals without violating others' limits.

Sigma Males Are Rare in Nature

While most individuals believe that demonstrating their dominance to others is the path to success, sigma males never look dominant. However, they will always convince you to do what they desire without your knowledge. If you want to succeed in a society where individuals might betray one another at the tiniest moment, you must constantly assume the worst of others. And because sigma males are prepared continuously, they are more likely to achieve success than other men.

However, sigma males never brag about their accomplishments and will continue pursuing their objectives without anyone noticing. And ladies will be fortunate to receive even a grin from this enigmatic and intriguing man. The sigma male likes making others believe they are his Sigma males are adept at obtaining whatever they desire without looking dominating or dominant, and this is one of the several reasons women find them appealing. They adore that this individual is quiet and possesses a strong personality. Sigma males are adept at using their intelligence and charisma to captivate women from a distance. Sigma males are calm and quiet, whereas alpha males are constantly noisy and dominant. They never boast about their accomplishments or attempt to impress others. To inform you, sigma males do not worry about anyone's validation. They are their greatest supporters, making them both romantically and professionally desirable. The sigma male is a breath of fresh air compared to the other males who want to intimidate others around them.

In brief, the sigma male may not be interested in demonstrating his strength, and he would allow other men to do it. Generally, women desire a sigma male because he understands when to be silent and allows others to talk endlessly about themselves.

Masculinity Rules that Make Sigma Males Outstanding

Have you ever questioned why sigma males are so distinguished in the manosphere?

Contrary to popular belief, Sigma males are not superhuman; they are men with extraordinary personalities and masculinity similar to yourself. They have learned the skills necessary to exist outside of social dominance hierarchies and to pursue their route in life.

They Learn to Shoulder the Burden

Sigma males are adept at solving problems. Regardless of how serious a situation appears, the sigma males will handle it and subconsciously lead everyone out of it. He may not be the leader, but he frequently assumes leadership responsibilities by proposing answers to difficult situations. And this comes with several responsibilities.

Sigma males do not avoid confrontations like Beta and omega males; they assume responsibility and guarantee everything is under control. Let's do this correctly. Sigma males do not attempt to impress others, so you won't see them striving to be heroes in other people's predicaments. But sigma males take responsibility for each event that develops in their lives and are in charge of bringing it under control. They will tackle the responsibility with promptness and determination. In managing a scenario in their lives, sigma males may occasionally make blunders. However, lone wolves do not panic over their errors. Instead, they gain knowledge and apply it to future endeavors.

They Gain New Knowledge

Sigma males have an unquenchable need for knowledge. And this facilitates their acquisition of wisdom. They always spend time alone, contemplate the world around them, strive to acquire new knowledge, and gain wisdom. Sigma males are not afraid of uncertainty. When required, they proceed into the Unknown without looking back. However, the unknown will undoubtedly terrify the average man as a beta male. Always seeking to improve themselves, lone wolves seek challenges and new experiences.

However, what precisely is the Unknown?

The Unknown is a facet of human psychology that is frequently avoided, and they continue to disregard it because it makes them feel uneasy. I'm referring to the inner demons that rule many individuals and hinder them from reaching their personal and professional objectives.

- It may be the dread of being rejected.
- The dread of public humiliation,
- The dread of abandonment,
- The fear of experiencing life alone,
- The worry about poverty,
- Prevalence of insecurity, and so on.

Interestingly, sigma males possess some of these demons. However, they always stare at the devils and confront them one by one. When any of these demons attempt to manipulate a lone wolf's mind, the lone wolves have a technique of regaining mental control. And the demons are helpless against the sigma males due to the constant removal of their fuel, which constitutes the human mind. Therefore, one of the masculine norms that makes sigma males so distinctive is that they constantly welcome the unknown. And the capacity of sigma males to dominate their brains makes them the most remarkable men in the manosphere. Sometimes, Sigma males attain enormous insight by observing the errors of others. Therefore, they always read.

Sigma Males Are Exceptionally Determined

Sigma males are very decisive. Once they conclude, they will adhere to it. Even when the sigma males make the incorrect choice, they attempt to rectify it. Sigma males would instead make a poor decision and learn from it than not decide. After making a choice, they reflect on their errors and are prepared for the next. Using this strategy, the sigma males will not be susceptible to decision-making anxiety or contempt. The ability to make judgments and act independently distinguishes sigma males from all men in the manosphere. It makes them prosperous, famous, and alluring to women.

Don't misunderstand! I'm not attempting to claim that Sigma males do not fail. But they never surrender. The lone wolf thinks that being alive provides a second opportunity for everything. Therefore, regardless matter how many rejections they receive, sigma males never lose hope. They will continue to try and try until the default answer is yes.

In a nutshell, the sigma males represent the progress of humanity. And because of the steps taken by some of the first sigma males, we now live in a better society. Sigma males are constantly in charge of their daily life, make rapid decisions, and take the initiative in a group by suggesting and choosing when they cannot.

Remember that sigma males are initiators and decision-makers for themselves and others.

Things Sigma Males Dislike

Sigma males enjoy being unconventional. This personality type is very inventive and less concerned with the fictitious social order. They have a penchant for rebellion and reinterpretation. Due to Sigma Male's inventiveness, they always come up with world-changing ideas and solutions. Typically, Sigma Males are inflexible and arrogant. And they are courageous; they are challenging to frighten. They cannot even operate efficiently in a conventional career system. Therefore, most Sigma males prefer to be independent contractors, entrepreneurs, and innovators. You will like Sigma Male's outlook on life. They are straightforward, devoted, empathetic, and intellectually curious.

If a sigma male finds himself in any system, he may immediately identify the system's logical flaws. However extraordinary this personality type may appear, they have its limitations. And once they are pushed to their breaking point, sigma males will not hesitate to strike back.

Continuous Social Interaction

Males of the Sigma species dislike needless social engagement and prefer their company to any other individual. A sigma Male will instead read a book, work on a project, develop an idea through brainstorming, or meditate than spend time with a social circle. Even if Sigma Male deeply loves you, he still requires his own space, and if you spend too much time with him, he's likely to give you attitude.

Do not misunderstand; Sigma Males like conversing with others. However, they prefer discussing subjects that are experts and pertinent to their career and personal development.

Therefore, do not anticipate your sigma male buddy participating in gossip or small talk with you. As soon as you attempt to add banal topics within the discussion, the sigma male will vanish.

Rules and Status Quo

Sigma Males strongly dislike following the rules. Consequently, they are frequently referred to as rule-breakers. If they operate in an organization, they challenge every rule, bend them, and occasionally break them when they discover superior alternatives. One thing that all sigma males dislike is maintaining the status quo. They are continually inventive, modifying, and searching for improved and simpler problem-solving methods. However, sigma males are typically quite dissatisfied if they work in an atmosphere discouraging creativity.

Routine Tasks

Since sigma males become bored easily, they dislike regular work. The optimal outcome cannot be achieved by delegating everyday work to sigma males. Whether the task is process-oriented or administrative, sigma males will not enjoy it. They attempt to make it enjoyable when required to perform a mundane duty. Every day, they will try to approach the procedure differently, even though it may be the same, and this may exacerbate the situation.

Being Forced to Deal with A Lot of Details

Sigma males depend heavily on their instincts. They are more productive at generating new ideas, developing inventive solutions, and solving problems. Sigma males are perpetually curious and able to perceive the larger picture in any scenario. They dislike dealing with several particulars. And forcing them to do it will not provide the greatest results.

Let's be clear: sigma males dislike managing many details does not mean they cannot handle them when essential. However, they are disinterested in any work that takes attention to minute details.

Lack of Time Alone

Even though Sigma Males are interested in other people, they are introverts who love spending time alone. When a sigma male doesn't get enough alone time, he becomes agitated and weary. Consequently, they will grow hostile and lose their patience. Again, if you are the cause of a sigma male not having sufficient time alone, he will detest you.

Pressure to Discuss Their Emotions

Extremely difficult for Sigma males to manage emotional stress. And due to their solitary nature, sigma males tend to keep their relationship and emotional problems to themselves. Even if they have heartbreak or other emotional challenges, they avoid discussing it with close friends. Sigma males cannot address emotional concerns. However, they require more processing time than other individuals. And they must feel secure with you before discussing their relationship problems. However, they find it incredibly frustrating when compelled to discuss their emotions and sentiments.

Compromising their Values

Sigma males adhere tenaciously to their ideals. No matter what is at stake, the sigma male never compromises his principles. This is likely due to his idealistic perspective on the world. Sigma Males have an innate understanding of how society, culture, and humanity should function. And nothing frustrates a sigma male more than when they are pressured to sacrifice their high moral values for a career or a relationship. They would gladly leave the position or relationship.

Ignorance

Sigma Males enjoy reading and learning. And if they know a great deal about a subject you don't know anything about, they will not make you feel inadequate. However, you will fall out with a sigma male if you express an opinion about an issue you know little about or if you criticize education.

Individuals Who Do Not Apply Their Knowledge

The Sigma Male is intellectually curious, and they are constantly eager to gain new knowledge. However, they do not simply acquire information; instead, they seek to apply it. They despise those who frequently generate brilliant ideas but never implement them. Even if you are close with a sigma male and he detects this feature, he will progressively separate himself from you.

Insincerity

Sigma males do not accept dishonesty. They despise dishonest individuals who are also dishonest with themselves. The sigma males are not perfect and occasionally make incorrect assumptions about others. However, they also believe in their intuitive hunches. Once they learn that you are dishonest with yourself or others, they will not hesitate to avoid you. A sigma male will always choose to have few trustworthy buddies over a large group of acquaintances.

Stagnant People

Sigma Males are constantly striving to improve themselves. And they cannot survive in a setting where individuals do not attempt to develop themselves. A sigma Male must improve themselves. And you cannot be friends with a sigma male if you wish to remain unchanged and not grow.

Criticism

Sigma males take every word seriously. Positive and encouraging comments will always soothe and inspire a sigma male, regardless of the circumstance. But unpleasant remarks may destroy a sigma male's entire day. He would feel unmotivated and uninspired and dwell on these negative thoughts for hours or days. Sigma males are aware that they are not flawless, and therefore, they welcome constructive feedback. However, how you give the feedback significantly impacts how a sigma male will perceive it.

People Who Never Give and Never Receive

It warms the heart of a sigma male to gratify others. And they always go over and above to make their loved ones happy. Typically, sigma males prioritize the needs of others before their own. However, they dislike it when you attempt to exploit their generosity. A sigma male feels irritated if he is the only one making sacrifices or if you do not appreciate his pleasant gestures towards you.

Confrontation

Sigma males dislike confrontation. Protracted fights, tension, and drama are detrimental to the health of the sigma males. When a sigma male has problems with their loved ones or frequent strain in their relationship, they may get physically ill. You can have a productive discourse with Sigma males even though they dislike conflict. Approach the matter courteously, and you will have a wonderful conversation.

When Life Is Devoid of Meaning

Every sigma male seeks a meaningful existence and does not desire a life of monotony. Therefore, they rarely accept a 9-to-5 job, regardless of the compensation. They like utilizing their innate abilities to solve complicated challenges and attempt to comprehend the universe.

Key Takeaways

- Sigma male dominates by not dominating. The calm domination of Sigma males is misinterpreted as weakness. However, this makes them more influential and powerful than those who desire fame and notoriety.

- While most individuals believe that demonstrating their dominance to others is the path to success, sigma males never look dominant. However, they will always convince you to do what they desire without your knowledge.

- Sigma males do not enjoy confrontations like Alpha and omega males; they assume responsibility and guarantee everything is under control.

- Sigma males have an unquenchable need for knowledge. And this facilitates their acquisition of wisdom. They always spend time alone, contemplate the world around them, strive to acquire new knowledge, and gain wisdom.

- Sigma males are very decisive. Once they conclude, they will adhere to it. Even when the sigma males make the incorrect choice, they attempt to rectify it. Sigma males would instead make a poor decision and learn from it than not decide.

- Sigma males do not accept dishonesty. They despise dishonest individuals who are also dishonest with themselves.

CHAPTER 3

BEING A SIGMA MALE

Being a Sigma Male in Today's Society

To be a sigma male in today's society, one must be truthful and vulnerable. Unfortunately, many males nowadays live in denial. Once you're not comfortable with a scenario, you shouldn't pretend to be. That is not sigma behavior; instead, it is stupidity. As a sigma male, expressing your emotions does not make you weak. Even if you intend to move on from a situation, you must still gently express your feelings.

There are many Beta and damaged men who pose as Sigma males. In reality, however, these individuals are either Narcissists or Dark empaths. Real sigma males have exceptional emotional control. They will not conceal their emotions even if they seem strong during difficult times. The lone wolf will communicate their feelings over a specific system or circumstance. They will not be upset and will act with the utmost composure. You cannot call yourself a real sigma male if you fear criticism while expressing your opinions or emotions. Suppressing your emotions is a formula for unhappiness, poor communication, and even health issues. The joy of being a sigma male is following your route through life. You do not have to be held captive by long-standing preconceptions or assumptions about society. Being a Sigma male gives you the confidence to communicate your views, feelings, and desires.

One of the reasons why sigma males stand out in the manosphere is because they live on honesty. Being a sigma male in today's culture also requires self-awareness and the ability to function as a much fuller and superior version of oneself. The sigma males constantly express their creative sides without fear of being belittled, ridiculed, or labeled as weak.

Ultimately, they don't care what other people think of them. Because of this, they always have less stress, less sadness, and greater long-term health. When a sigma male is in a group, he is often called Mr Fix-it. Due to their creativity, they can tackle issues, and obstacles others deem impossible. In contemporary culture, being a sigma male also entails having a purpose. Sigma males feel that a man without a clear life goal is entirely lost, wandering, and reacting to events rather than creating them. When a male is unaware of his life's purpose, he lives a life of weakness and impotence. Regardless of the male energy you possess, it will be stifled if you do not define its purpose and put it to use. And when this occurs, it causes you and everyone around you irritation, wrath, and suffering. It is simple to unify your male traits and fundamental values under one roof when you have a goal. The simplest method to uncover your purpose is to be true to yourself, establish your worth, and determine what is so vital to you.

In a nutshell, modern sigma males embrace good masculinity and can utilize their physical and emotional power to promote healthy behaviors and practices. Sigma males are aware that they are imperfect and demonstrate their vulnerability, emotional intelligence, and moral strength. Remember that being a sigma male implies being truthful with oneself and talking authentically and without apology. Sigma males are the progress of humanity and the gods of men.

Sigma Vs Other Social Hierarchy Personalities

You have already learned that sigma and alpha males have many similarities. However, you may be curious about other personality types such as Betas, Omegas, and Deltas. To better understand the other personality types, examining their similarities and differences with the sigma personality is advisable.

Sigma Males Vs Alpha Males

Similarities: Sigma and Alpha males are confident and capable of accomplishing their goals, making them both influential leaders.

Differences: While alpha men are frequently dominant, sigma males avoid leadership positions while being the best suited to challenge alpha males for social dominance.

Sigma Males Vs Beta Males

Similarities: These two personality types are noted for their quiet demeanor and indifference to remaining in the background.

Differences: Sigma and beta males are content with being alone, but the latter also enjoys belonging to a group. A sigma male dislikes participating in social hierarchies, distinguishing them from beta men. Sometimes, beta males are labeled as bottom-feeders, but this is just because Sigma's are more self-aware.

Sigma Males Vs Omega Males

Similarities: Both Sigma and omega males possess confidence and independence.

Differences: Sigma males are often alone and emotionally independent, whereas omega males maintain a small network of friends for emotional support.

Sigma Males Vs Delta Males

Similarities: a male delta is occasionally called a lone wolf.

Differences: Sigma males refuse to join the pack. They choose to walk away from the social dominance hierarchy. On the other hand, Delta males thrive within the stable framework of social dominance hierarchy. The more stable this hierarchy is the better it becomes for the delta way of life.

How to Become a Sigma Male

Now, you will know whether or not you are a Sigma Male. If you are a Sigma, you likely wish to confirm a suspicion. Probably a friend requested that you read this book on your own, though you care nothing about labels. If you are not already a Sigma, you may be interested in joining. Who would not want to become a mysterious and alluring version of the Alpha?

Nowadays, countless Alphas are competing for the top spot. However, years of experience are required to become one. And as you can see, it is not always anticipated for school males to materialize as Sigmas. People expect males to behave a certain way, yet some boys take a quiet position at a young age. You cannot force yourself to be a Sigma, but you may likely awaken the Sigma within you.

Here are several methods for incorporating Sigma character:

- Recognize yourself. Recognize that you do not always need to be the focal point.
- Practice disregarding the opinions of others.
- If you are pretending to be a Beta, remove that mask. You can be quietly confident.
- Choose your companions carefully. Stick to the select few.
- Learn to pay attention. When you do so, you discover that you learn more this way than through conversation.
- Be self-reliant. Develop abilities that will improve your ability to survive on your own.
- Connect with your inner self more. Spend some time in contemplation and meditation.

How Sigma Male Handle Anger - Sigma Male Emotions

For most people, falling in love is mostly a matter of feelings and emotions. However, falling in love might be challenging for a sigma male, and this is due to their need to apply rationality to all situations, including relationships. Therefore, sigma males have their thoughts on their soul mates when locating them, and occasionally, they may even be somewhat cynical about it. Feelings and romance challenge the sigma male since they are more attracted to proven facts and evidence.

What is A Soulmate to A Sigma Male?

A sigma male might not believe in soulmates due to their rational nature and emphasis on evidence-based matters above emotions. Intriguingly, the concept of a soulmate extends beyond emotional notions such as love and compatibility. And when a sigma male eventually accepts the idea of a soulmate, he views it quite differently than a more romantically inclined one. Having a soulmate has nothing to do with love to a sigma male; instead, you are paired with someone based on their distinct attributes. From the perspective of a sigma male, this indicates that you are likely to have more than one soul mate or perfect match. To a sigma male, the notion that there is only one person in the world suited for you is ridiculous and appears implausible and fictitious.

A sigma male views soulmates as those who inspire and challenge them to be the most refined version of themselves, someone who has a profound grasp of the characteristics of the sigma male can connect with their soul in a way that no one else can. The sigma male certainly believes in love.

The Rational Sigma Male Mind and Romance

People often believe that the sigma male is uninteresting and unromantic. It is not always the case. They are pretty reasonable and rational in all situations. However, they may also be somewhat romantic and comprehend how to make their spouses feel loved and cherished. Even though some sigma males may shy away from romance, there are a few highly amorous ones. They are honest with themselves. A sigma male cannot commit time and romantic energy to someone for whom they do not have real sentiments and intentions.

A sigma male is not obligated to act amorously towards another person simply because they choose to be. And many sigma males possess a lyrical quality. Therefore, they can articulate their sentiments when they are attracted to someone. Interestingly, many sigma males desire sexual relationships. And they want to find someone with whom they can truly share their life. However, they frequently struggle to balance their passionate side and their extremely rational intellect. Because they believe in verifiable facts, they may apply the same standard to their relationships. Therefore, they employ pragmatic criteria while selecting a soulmate or life companion.

When a sigma male gets to know someone and recognizes the actual potential of their relationship, he will consult a compatibility checklist to see how compatible he is with this person. They will study the individual's character and other pertinent information to determine whether they can be in a genuine connection with that person.

This approach to relationships may strike you as chilly and unromantic. But for a sigma male, it indicates that they are committed to the individual. Moreover, he may be pondering spending the rest of his life with this someone. However, once a sigma male no longer sees a future with a person, he dislikes wasting their time. Again, it is always difficult for the sigma male to establish a balance between their rational and passionate thinking. And they must maintain this equilibrium; otherwise, their connection would always be problematic. Even though sigma males like using information and results before a relationship, they must also know when to express emotion.

In addition, they should learn to pay attention to their intuition when it tells them to be vulnerable and connect with the person they love. Surprisingly, the few sigma males who are more successful at discovering their genuine soul mate and true love are those who pay attention to their intuition and instinct. In relationships, he must learn to be less logical and more emotional. When the sigma male meets the appropriate spouse, that person will be patient enough to wait till they open up. However, sigma males still need to learn how to analyze their relationships with less reasoning and more passion. They must be open to love and find someone they can truly confide in. However, after a sigma male determines that he can trust you, he progressively removes some of his barriers. Again do not rush into anything or immediately reveal their feelings to someone they adore.

Nevertheless, sigma males must occasionally allow themselves to take risks. The sigma male may never attain his relationship objective until he offers himself the chance to meet his ideal partner. Contrary to popular belief, opening out is only part of the journey for a sigma male to meet a soul mate.

What The Sigma Male Needs

Sigma male is passionate about those who understand him more profoundly. A sigma male will always prioritize someone who understands them above all others, regardless of their flaws. Every sigma male needs a partner who understands their need for privacy and does not take it personally. This personality type values a partner who appreciates their preference for solitude. Even if the sigma male does not verbally express their feelings to them, they are still significant in their life.

As you already know, sigma males are not naturally overly emotional or sentimental. Therefore, they require a patient and appreciative partner of their true intentions. They do not desire stagnation; therefore, they want their partner to help them grow and challenge them uniquely.

The sigma male needs a companion who ignites his heart, soul, and mind—a person who can challenge their intelligence and cause them to view things from a fresh angle. The sigma males require a mate who is not just brilliant but also empathetic toward them—someone who enables them to perceive other aspects of themselves, not only the image they present to the world. The sigma male also desires someone loyal and willing to stick with them regardless of the future. The genuine soulmate of a sigma male will be understanding and encouraging and always be truthful with him, even when it is difficult. The sigma male needs someone who is patient and does not continually smooth them. They require time alone, expecting their spouse or soulmate to understand their reasons.

One area in which the sigma male is frequently misinterpreted is his hate of other people. However, this is not accurate. The sigma male occasionally needs to be alone to enable them to ponder and generate original ideas. However, this does not imply that they do not care or desire to be near their loved ones. Once you cannot see why a sigma male requires alone time, he will begin to detest any contact with you. Therefore, the soul mate of a sigma male is someone who respects his alone time without making him feel bad—someone who can be close to Sigma and make him feel loved while respecting his desire for solitude.

In addition, the soul partner of sigma males must be able to comprehend the intricacy of their minds. The individual must embrace his characteristics and refrain from judging the sigma male's efforts to see things from a new perspective. The sigma male needs a partner who adores his heart, spirit, and controversial and distinctive characteristics. When required, the sigma male falls hopelessly in love with anyone who is both warm and reasonable. Let me clarify: the sigma male dislikes partners who are identical to themselves. Instead, people want to be with someone who shares some of their activities. Surprisingly, the sigma males are eager to share themselves with others. That is, they desire to fall in love with somebody. They desire someone with whom they can share their difficulties. And someone who will lend a helping hand when times are tough. Unfortunately, the process is not simple for them. The sigma male requires patience and a spouse who does not always misunderstand his goals in a relationship.

Additionally, the sigma male values honesty in a relationship and is pretty serious about it. No matter how much a sigma male loves his spouse, the relationship will never be the same once he detects honesty. The sigma male is ecstatic when he meets someone who is straightforward and does not hide things due to their emotions. Once a sigma male discovers someone who fully comprehends them, they develop a profound affection for that individual. A relationship requires a partner who looks beyond the surface—someone who cherishes their individuality and the fact that they perceive the world differently than everyone else.

Reasons Sigma Males Never Feel Empty

A sigma male is an individual, and his life is neither impacted nor governed by the movements of others around him. Sigma males live autonomously, put themselves first, and never seek the spotlight. They take pleasure in spending time alone and contemplating the world around them. This explains why they are consistently driven and enthusiastic in all circumstances. Regardless of the events, sigma males never experience emptiness. They value their lives above everything else and are conscious of their routines. Sigma males will never conform to the expectations of others. You are not worthy of becoming their buddy if you cannot accept them for who they are.

This section discusses four reasons why sigma males never feel empty. Unlike the majority of individuals, sigma males are not lonely. Sigma males get happier the more time they spend alone. A sigma male who feels lost or bewildered in his life does not panic, and all he needs is time alone to think, contemplate, and regain his energy.

They Possess a High Degree of Self-Awareness

Typically, people experience emptiness because they do not know who they are. When you lack self-awareness, you may experience emptiness. And this is because you feel your life lacks direction and meaning. However, sigma males possess an elevated sense of self-awareness. They are aware of who they are and have an understanding of their inner selves. Due to their self-awareness, sigma males never lose touch with who they are and what they desire and aspire to be. And because of this, lone wolves always have a purpose in life and never live to impress others. Every once in a while, sigma males escape the stresses of daily life and spend quality time alone. Individuals consider their innermost thoughts, emotions, values and beliefs during such times. This frequently assists children in establishing a solid sense of identity.

They Do Not Center Their Lives on Relationships

Because Sigma males are deeply aware of human nature, they do not base their lives on relationships. Sigma males seldom fall in love; even if they do, they attempt to remain sensible. Whether you are a friend or a romantic partner, sigma males constantly create limits in their interactions. Their happiness depends on their capacity to meditate and reflect on the world, not their relationships. Sigma males always develop significant relationships with others but do not center their lives on these relationships.

Occasionally, sigma males may have a few trustworthy friends with whom they may confide. But wolves anticipate the worse and hope for the best whenever lone wolves interact with humans.

They Always Make Peace with Their Past

Sigma males make peace with their past. Whether a sigma male has experienced loss, separation, or failure in the past, they always move on with their lives. Sigma males never revisit their pasts, and their attention and focus are always on the present moment. Sigma males know that previous events are over; grief cannot return them, melancholy cannot put things right, and misery cannot resurrect the past. This is because the past does not exist. Therefore, lone wolves are always present; they forgive themselves and permit themselves to develop and heal from whatever they have endured in the past.

They Always Have Aspirations and Dream

Sigma males never feel empty because they constantly have lofty aims and dreams. Therefore, they find purpose in every part of their lives because they have goals and objectives. The hopes and aspirations of the sigma males remind them that they have a significant function in life. And because they constantly contemplate their aspirations, they never find life monotonous and devoid.

Key Takeaways

- Being a sigma male in today's culture requires self-awareness and the ability to function as a much fuller and superior version of oneself.

- Sigma males embrace good masculinity and can utilize their physical and emotional power to promote healthy behaviors and practices.

- When a sigma male gets to know someone and recognizes the actual potential of their relationship, he will consult a compatibility checklist to see how compatible he is with this person.

- Every sigma male needs a partner who understands their need for privacy and does not take it personally.

- The sigma male needs a companion who ignites his heart, soul, and mind—a person who can challenge their intelligence and cause them to view things from a fresh angle.

CHAPTER 4

SIGMA MALE PSYCHOLOGY

Reasons People Can't Ignore the Sigma Males

Sigma males are enigmas. They cannot be ignored in a team or environment. People listen anytime they talk, and their wishes are granted when they ask. You cannot simply disregard the sigma males. Spending time with sigma males will leave you wondering why they are so charming. It's not magic. People treat sigma males differently and with respect because they have proven their worth. They have creative thoughts and superb poise, and they uniquely handle problems.

They Pay Attention to Others

One of the reasons people cannot overlook sigma males is that they pay attention to others during conversations. When conversing with a sigma male, he will listen attentively before speaking. No matter how stressful a situation may appear, sigma males never hurry to speak. They take the time to listen to everyone participating in the discussion and develop an original viewpoint that will wow everyone. Sigma males are unlike Alpha and Beta males, who spend their time talking about themselves. However, the fact that a sigma male consistently listens to others throughout a discussion provides the sense that he values their perspective. Even if they have a lot to say, lone wolves will listen to others first, regardless of how much they say.

They Seldom Critique

Sigma males have no patience for criticism. They live outside the social framework of society, dance to the beat of their drum, and pursue their path in life. Sigma males seldom criticize others. Even if you are doing something wrongly, sigma males will permit you to learn from your mistakes. Even if your criticism is well-intentioned, people will avoid you if it becomes excessive. When it is essential for a sigma male to criticize, he does it using a combination of encouragement and praise. With this method, individuals can always discern the critique's positive meaning.

They Are Upbeat Individuals

Sigma males are optimistic individuals who resist negativity and doubt at all costs. Even though they are experiencing difficulty, they maintain optimism. Sigma males think terrible circumstances do not last, but challenging individuals do. Sigma males strive to be a source of positivity whenever they are in a group. When everyone else is discouraged and ready to quit, the sigma male sees a million reasons to continue.

Their Presence Commands Notice

Let's get this straight: sigma males do not desire attention and try to avoid headlines. However, their presence always commands notice. Even when meeting the sigma males for the first time, you will be drawn to what he says, how he says it, and how he conducts himself in a group. Their self-assurance is unshakeable, and their public presentation is impeccable. Multiple studies indicate that people naturally attract and pay more attention to confident individuals. And the confidence of sigma males helps them subconsciously generate a favorable first impression. Their body language is appropriate, and they have a good outlook.

They Do Not Overthink What They Will Say

Sigma males have matured that what to say during a conversation comes effortlessly. They always know what to say in any given circumstance. They do not overthink topics before speaking, which is one reason why people cannot just ignore him. Stigma guys will be significantly engaged once a conversation is stimulating and cognitively taxing. Once conversing about something relevant and valuable, they can engage in a lengthy conversation with you. However, they avoid small talk at all costs, and he will avoid you if you constantly engage in diminutive conversation with the sigma male. Sigma males are essentially who they are. They do not alter themselves to attract individuals. This is one of the reasons why individuals cannot ignore them. They find lone wolves amazing.

Ways Silence Makes the Sigma Males More Powerful

Sigma males understand the power of silence, which explains why they may be in a place for an extended period without speaking. They may not be pleased with what is happening around them, but lone wolves do not respond instantly to problems. Before speaking, they try to examine every facet of the circumstance. If you've studied

Robert Greene's The 48 Laws of Power, you'll realize why sigma males always say less than required.

This section will explain the five ways the sigma male's silence makes them more powerful. One thing is sure: lone wolves understand when to remain silent and when not to. However, they do not respond emotionally to difficulties and are therefore highly respected.

They Appear More Powerful When They Are Silent

By speaking less, sigma males subconsciously impress and frighten others. Since lone wolves comprehend the human mind, they know that the more they speak, the more foolish they would appear. It is impossible to observe sigma males bragging about their accomplishments or greatness. And once a sigma male observes someone blowing their own horn, he understands that the individual is either a narcissist or a liar.

Some of history's greatest sigma males are recognized for speaking little, and their silence has historically been the basis of their authority. Even if the sigma male is not the team leader, his silence gives the impression that he is more powerful. And occasionally more influential than the leader himself. Because sigma males speak less frequently, their words have more weight. Sigma males are mysterious and elusive because they always say less than is required.

They Can Read Individuals Through Silence

Silence enables sigma males to listen and monitor others constantly. It makes it easier for lone wolves to identify liars and discern individuals' genuine motives. When the sigma male remains silent, he can watch people's body language and determine if it coincides with what they say. The sigma males acquire the capacity to read individuals via quiet.

You Cannot Take Back Wrong Words

Whatever the sigma males say, they carefully consider it before uttering it. The lone wolves are incredibly cautious with their words to avoid uttering anything they would later regret. The sigma males attain a great level of self-control through silence. Sigma males can maintain self-control and rarely strike out at others, regardless of their circumstances. Even if you smack a sigma male in public, he may not instantly respond. And this is because he knows that it is not worth it to respond instantly. The lone wolves know one fact: servicing your ego distances you from the things you desire in life. Regardless of the situation, sigma males will always keep their mouths shut, remain calm, and stand their ground in silence. Instead of expressing their feelings, sigma males always respond strategically.

Silence Makes Them Excellent Listeners

Have you ever wondered why individuals like conversing with sigma males so much? They are excellent listeners. When you listen to others, they will like conversing with you. The sigma males comprehend that individuals desire to be heard and understood. And being silent and attentive throughout a discussion helps others feel wonderful. Because of this, sigma males look more charming while in a group.

They Employ Silence as an Effective Negotiating Tool

Sigma males utilize quiet to persuade the other side during negotiations. Once a sigma male negotiates in silence, he often has the upper hand once he speaks. Silence during negotiations indicates that the other party requires the sigma male more than he requires them.

Subtle Habits That Make Sigma Males Mentally Strong

Sigma males are renowned for their mental toughness and lack of fear, and they never permit fear to deprive them of their aspirations. At all times, sigma males exhibit mental strength and perseverance, making it easier for them to attain their goals. Due to their mental toughness, sigma males always unlock the door to courage. And even when severe life storms strike sigma males, they never experience depression or anxiety. The lone wolf recognizes that suffering is a part of existence. Consequently, they are constantly psychologically prepared to manage these pains' emotional triggers and negative ideas.

They Are in Control of Their Emotions

Sigma males have a great level of emotional control. Regardless of their emotions, they do not respond to difficulties with naivety. They may be irritated, apprehensive, and sometimes furious. These emotions do not render sigma males fragile. However, sigma males do not permit these feelings to govern them, and they attempt to maintain emotional control and manage the issue with maturity. This explains why sigma males will not physically attack others during a dispute. They will maintain composure while being unhappy. Even when depressed, the sigma male does not let his emotions impact those around him. And this is because he has emotional control. Sigma males identify negative feelings when they experience them and understand how to overcome these emotional obstacles.

They Question All Ideas and Beliefs

Sigma males do not consider every opinion or belief they have. The lone wolf always pushes themselves by analyzing their thoughts and beliefs critically. They constantly question the authenticity of any information. Regardless of the source of information, sigma males do not accept everything they hear as fact. Because sigma males are intellectually robust, they question or analyze everything they encounter. No matter who informed them or where they read it, sigma males will verify all information twice before accepting it. And the fact that sigma males question things allows them to learn more and gives them the chance to understand the perspectives of others. This provides people control over the impact of the information they receive.

They Establish Healthy Boundaries for Themselves

Establishing healthy boundaries is a behavior that makes sigma males mentally strong. Regardless of your relationship with the sigma male, he will always set his limits. The lone wolf must never allow others to use him as a doormat. The capacity of sigma males to establish healthy boundaries with the people in their lives enhances their mental power.

In reality, a person's self-respect is reflected in their limits, indicating how others should regard you and allow you to be your best self. And since they lack limits, Beta and Omega males always say yes to everyone, even when it's inconvenient. Even though sigma males want to be there for the people in their lives, they cannot constantly be at everyone's beck and call since doing so would bring them unneeded stress.

They Learn from Their Mistakes

The lone wolves never become obsessed with their past actions because it would simply increase their stress levels. The sigma male considers what occurred, investigates why it happened, and devises a strategy to prevent it in the future. The sigma males will grow mentally robust due to recognizing their mistakes, learning from them, and figuring out how to prevent them in the future.

They Seldom Engage On Social Media

Social media plays a significant role in modern life. And many individuals base their whole lives on social media. Social media is a wonderful method to stay in touch with family and friends. However, sigma males are not social media addicts. They are aware that excessive use of social media encourages individuals to compare their lives to those of others. The feeling that the grass is greener on the other side might be induced by other people's filtered, glossy images and social media postings about their alleged pleasant life. Sigma males know this and spend less time on social networking networks. According to studies, chronic usage of social networking sites and apps may be associated with depressive symptoms. It causes individuals to believe they are inadequate. However, sigma males recognize that spending less time on social media might aid in avoiding depression-inducing comparisons.

Ways Sigma Males Spot Fake Nice People

Sigma males despise fake good people. They look kind in your presence yet speak negatively about you when you are not around. The lone wolves do not take these individuals' praises seriously since, in actuality, they do not have the sigma males' best interests in mind. Sigma males do not seek the approval of others. And he does not care if your kindness towards them is genuine.

Humble Bragging

One of how sigma males identify phony nice individuals is through humble bragging, a circumstance in which someone displays fake humility. These individuals tend to give others the idea that they minimize their achievements. In actuality, though, they are boasting about them. For example, it is humble bragging for someone to declare, "I detest being affluent because people always beg me for money." Sigma males appreciate someone who brags authentically about their accomplishments over someone who boasts modestly.

Passive Aggressive Behavior

Once a sigma male observes passive-aggressive conduct in others, he makes every effort to avoid them. People that engage in passive-aggressive conduct are extremely hostile yet appear nice and friendly. Sigma males know that persons with this conduct have previously attempted to control their wrath. They continually strive to preserve decorum and class. In addition, they communicate their anger through passive-aggressive conduct. Sigma males dislike those who are not like themselves. And once people detect your passive-aggressive conduct, they instantly avoid you. Sigma males would prefer to be friendless than to have fake friends.

Fake Emotions

One thing that turns off sigma males is faking emotions. Fake emotions might manifest in various ways, and they might be feigned regret, melancholy, etc. And soon, sigma males discover that someone is attempting to influence them with phony emotions, and they avoid that person. Because sigma males have such a deep understanding of human emotions, they can immediately detect someone faking their feelings. And sometimes, the emotions make no sense, and they express them in the most extreme manner possible, making them easier to identify for sigma males.

They Like Slandering and Criticizing Others

The usual conduct of fake nice people is constantly pulling others down to become close to you. When a sigma male observes individuals behaving this way, he understands they are pretenders. Therefore, he avoids them at all costs. Every fake nice person you encounter enjoys gossiping in a way that makes them appear kind. Occasionally, they may even exhibit a fake feeling of care for what others are experiencing. This conduct may be difficult for others to recognize. However, because of the wise nature of sigma males, they can immediately identify fake nice people anytime they display fake feelings for the misery of others.

They Cannot Listen

Sigma males dislike individuals who cannot listen. People who are constantly eager to discuss themselves in a gathering. If you cannot listen while others talk, sigma males will view you as insincere. This is because genuine friends would listen to you no matter what you are going through. However, because fake friendly people are self-centered, it will be difficult for them to sit down and listen to others. The slogan of a fake nice person is "I, myself, and I." The focus is on them, and they will always play the role and finally steer the discourse in their favor.

They Always Want Something

Have you ever wondered why phony people are always courteous and kind? They are requesting something from you and attempt not to make it too clear initially. They will converse with you normally but gradually direct the conversation towards what they want from you. Sigma males recognize that fake nice individuals constantly desire to be on the receiving end. They desire something from you or want you to perform a service for them. Therefore, as sigma males realize the true motivations behind their behaviors, they begin to shun them as though they were a plague.

They Are Only Polite to Powerful Individuals

Sigma males may spot a fake individual because he is only polite to people in authority who can aid to help him. And often, sigma males can rapidly determine a great deal about your character based on how you treat others who are less wealthy or less powerful than you. But you are a phony if you only aim your good energy and nice demeanor toward people in authority. And none of the friendly acts you display toward these individuals is real. These are the seven ways sigma males detect phony individuals.

Self-sabotaging Behavior Sigma Males Always Avoid

Sigma males possess a great degree of self-awareness. They are attuned to what is occurring within them, from their thoughts and emotional responses to how they manage difficult situations. Because sigma males pay attention to their most profound ideas, climbing the success ladder is simple.

Often, people unwittingly obstruct their progress toward their objectives. People participate in these self-destructive behaviors without even being aware of them. This section will describe the seven self-destructive behaviors that all sigma males avoid.

Meaning of Self-Sabotage

Self-Sabotaging conduct is any action that inhibits an individual from accomplishing their goals. People self-sabotage most of the time out of fear of failure, change, and leaving their comfort zone. Sigma males see the risk of self-destructive conduct and avoid it.

Procrastination

One of the self-destructive activities that sigma males usually avoid is procrastination. After establishing a goal, a sigma male exerts persistent effort to attain it, and he makes every effort to prevent procrastination from occurring. Regardless of the obstacles, sigma males do not veer from their objectives. The sigma males know that inaction will prevent them from achieving their objectives. So, after establishing a goal, they instantly begin taking action until it is achieved.

Negative Self-Talk

Negative self-talk is one of the most challenging forms of self-sabotage. It refers to any self-talk that inhibits a person's ability to believe in themselves and their abilities and realize their full potential. Sigma males recognize the dangers associated with negative self-talk. Because of this, they avoid any notion that undermines their capacity to make positive changes or might impair their self-confidence. Therefore, sigma males constantly tell themselves that no objective is unattainable.

It makes no difference how often the sigma male fails. Irrespective of how frequently they face hurdles, they never engage in negative self-talk. Once a sigma male has established his goals, he strives to eliminate any inner debate that might potentially impede them from accomplishing their objectives. The lone wolf thinks that your life experiences reflect your ideas. Once you feel that you cannot perform anything, your mind will be trained to act accordingly. And as a result, you will lose interest in that activity and be unable to complete it.

Staying in Their Comfort Zone

Staying in one's comfort zone is one of the self-destructive behaviors that sigma males avoid. The lone wolves know that the comfort zone is a psychological condition in which individuals feel familiar, secure, and at ease. Most people in this zone do not wish to take actions that will alter their lives, which explains why most individuals fear change. But the reality is that you cannot alter your life unless you leave your comfort zone. The guys of Sigma believe that transformation begins at the edge of one's comfort zone, and people may only begin to live the life of their dreams after leaving their comfort zone.

Not Attending to Their Physical Health

Sigma males are diligent and clever. However, they take their health extremely seriously. They consistently recharge their bodies, obtain sufficient rest, engage in physical activities, and pay great attention to their physical health. Because sigma males pay special attention to their physical health, they are constantly emotionally, cognitively, and physically balanced. If you neglect your physical health, you cannot function at a high level. And once you cannot perform optimally, you are less likely to achieve your objectives.

Lack of Concern for Mental Health

Sigma males do not jeopardize their mental health. No matter how busy they are, they prioritize their mental health. Your mental health includes your emotional, psychological, and social well-being, influencing your thoughts, feelings, and actions. When a person's mental health is optimal, they can effectively manage stress, interact with others, and make wise decisions. Because sigma males recognize the importance of mental health throughout all stages of life, from infancy and adolescence to maturity, they pay great attention to it. If your mental health is poor, you cannot concentrate and achieve your objectives.

Blaming Others for Misfortunes

Sigma males always accept responsibility. Regardless of what occurred, they do not hold anyone accountable. They are aware that horrible things can occur without anyone's fault. Indeed, inevitable catastrophes may be attributed to the actions of others, but this is not always the case. Instead of blaming others when things go awry, sigma males examine their contributions to the misfortune. Thus, they can identify the issue and implement the necessary changes.

Dating Individuals Who Are Not Suitable for Them

Relationships are another domain in which self-destructive habits manifest. But sigma males will always avoid dating unsuitable individuals. Regardless of how attractive a woman may appear, sigma males will not want to date her if she does not meet all their requirements. This explains why sigma males won't strive to make a relationship work with a partner with different future aspirations or stay in a relationship that isn't progressing. If a sigma male desires children, he will not date a partner who does not and vice versa.

Ways Sigma Males Make Their Life More Positive

Sigma males always have an optimistic lifestyle. Regardless of the situation, lone wolves concentrate more on solutions than problems. They are continually looking to better themselves and their life. They learn from their mistakes, move on, and attempt again with a different strategy. Certainty dictates that sigma males never linger on the past; they always make the most of the present.

This section will explore the eleven ways sigma males improve their lives.

They Consistently Avoid Toxic Relationships and Individuals

By avoiding toxic friends and individuals, Sigma males may make their lives more positive. No matter how close you are to the sigma male, he will avoid you at all costs if you are toxic. The sigma male would prefer to be alone than be in a relationship with someone who treats them as a convenience or an item.

Addiction

Sigma males may have flaws, but they are not addicted. They may smoke and take alcohol but are never addicted. The lone wolves feel that being an addict is not the only way to live, and they would rather confront their difficulties than use addiction to escape them.

Hobby

Every sigma male has a hobby. During their spare time, they concentrate and enjoy it

Career

Sigma males are incredibly picky about their career and shun any job that does not make them happy, regardless of the compensation. The lone wolves are constantly interested in exploring life and pursuing a fulfilling profession, and they begin by investigating their passion and conceiving a means to profit from it.

Expectations

Sigma males do not live a life of expectation and know that expectations can lead to failure and dissatisfaction. The sigma males always accept life and respond to things in a nonreactive manner.

Wellness

Sigma males constantly look out for themselves and monitor their diet and exercise at least five times every week.

Goals

Sigma males take their goals and objectives very seriously. They set daily, weekly, monthly, and annual targets and endeavor to make these goals and objectives feasible and pursue their attainment. The more sigma males accomplish their objectives, the more their confidence and feeling of purpose.

They Care Less About Other People's Opinion

Sigma males do not live to impress others and could care less what other people think of them. They engage in activities that provide them joy and a feeling of purpose. They have such confidence in themselves that they disregard the opinions of others.

Self-Awareness

Sigma males possess a great degree of self-awareness. They consistently exercise control over their ideas, emotions, and behaviors, which explains why they always lead happy lives.

They Read a Lot

In general, sigma males like gaining new knowledge and are always interested in reading about unfamiliar topics. As a result, the sigma males have knowledge on a lot of topics.

How Sigma Males Control Fear Through Masculinity

Due to their high level of masculinity, sigma males are singular and uncommon in contemporary culture. Lone wolves possess male energy but also know how to unleash and utilize it. This explains why sigma males may readily become the focus of attention in any setting, despite their attempts to remain calm and quiet.

Fear and masculinity are mortal adversaries that cannot coexist in a man, and one must prevail over another. Either fear or masculinity predominates. For most males, particularly the Beta and Omega Males, fear invariably trumps their manhood. Over time, they acquire a severe aversion to danger and a poor sense of self-worth. However, sigma males are conscious of the continual struggle between their masculinity and anxiety for domination.

Therefore, they attempt to engage their masculine energy and learn how to take creative initiative when other guys might panic. Sigma males do not permit fear to stifle their masculinity; instead, they use their masculinity to control fear. Whenever fear threatens to derail the sigma males' attempts to attain their goals, they overcome it and find a method to revive their manly vitality. The lone wolves know that fear is a hasty conclusion of an undisciplined mind based on partial truths and erroneous information. And those who allow this undisciplined aspect of their thinking to affect them tend to become weak and indecisive, damaging their masculinity. People in this group tend to live on autopilot and view themselves as inferior in the presence of other males. Surprisingly, the powerful masculine intellect of sigma males allows them to influence those around them readily.

The sigma males are fearless regardless of how difficult the circumstance appears and how uncertain the future appears. They think that fear is an illusion that appears to be accurate and a misleading emotion that might undermine all of your hard work. It's rather amusing that people frequently create unneeded difficulties for something that may never occur. The sigma males know that such acts might impair their judgment and diminish their macho vigor over time.

Do not misunderstand; sigma males are not superheroes. Over time, however, they have trained their minds to view things for what they are, without fear. Every sigma male has a different perspective on fear; they feel that fear is a fraud with no factual basis. The lone wolves feel that fear is a shadow attempting to become legitimate. Analyze all the occasions in which you were so terrified in the past. But because you give your mind so much power, you make dread real by paying too much attention. The sigma males think that when your dread materializes, it is because you gave it your complete attention. Therefore, sigma males do not concern themselves with anything beyond their control. They just accept the existence of the difficulty and recognize it for what it is.

The sigma males know that fear is a scam artist disguised as a police officer. However, if you recognize fear for what it is, it will have little to no power over you. However, embracing your fear does not necessitate recklessness; it is by gathering bravery and accepting obstacles to progress. Sigma males know that genuine fear is much different from psychological anxiety. For example, seeing a hungry lion on the street is real, yet imagining and being terrified of what may occur in the future is not psychological or real. They are shadows with no actual power unless you cultivate them over time.

In a word, sigma males view fear as a fraud that cannot exist unless it receives attention. Due to their masculinity, sigma males find fear useless and insignificant. Therefore, sigma males do not give terror power since they recognize that fear is their domain and cannot exist without their permission. As soon as you realize that fear is meaningless without your consent, it has no power over you.

And when that occurs, you will regain your self-assurance and become the master of your life.

Why Sigma Male's Are Emotionally Stable

The emotional stability of sigma males is puzzling. Even if they have a rough day or face significant obstacles, they maintain their composure. The lone wolves are life-realistic, knowing that not everything is perfect and that things do not always go as planned. Sigma males view setbacks and obstacles as components of what makes life exciting. They are not like the average man, obsessed with overly optimistic aspirations.

Most men today desire to be happier, healthier, and superior to others. People desire to be smarter, quicker, wealthier, sexier, more popular, productive, envious and adored. These men have quite bizarre fantasies regarding our planet. They want to fly their helicopter to their satisfying work, where they spend their days saving the globe.

All of your good and wonderful life dreams are fixated on the things you lack. And when you expect to have everything at your beck and call, you tend to be upset when things do not go your way. This might have psychological, physical, and emotional effects on you. But sigma males have a unique worldview and a different outlook on life.

They are aware of countless terrible experiences for every fantastic event a person has. There were numerous unrecorded failures for every triumph that was recorded. Life is replete with uncertainties, and Sigma males know this reality and desire to experience life as it unfolds on occasion. This clarifies why sigma males are emotionally stable.

This book is for you if you have ever wondered why Lone wolves are emotionally stable and focused regardless of the scenario. Every sigma male is aware of one fact: they control their world. Most individuals may find this difficult to accept. Nevertheless, some of the greatest men in history are those who find methods to build their world. They have influenced over 80% of the events in their lives. Sigma males would instead alter their lives than moan about them. The lone wolf comprehends emotional psychology. And they are aware that people offer their emotional strength unknowingly to external factors. Over time, these forces will activate these individuals' emotions and transform them into their worst selves. However, sigma males are not emotionally triggered by external circumstances and maintain emotional control regardless of the circumstances.

The sigma males live a life devoid of ego and unwarranted anxiety, providing inner calm and emotional stability. The sigma males know that ego is a destructive feeling capable of destroying anything, and it can launch a war, wipe out a tribe, and torch a nation. Even while the ego is a survival mechanism, it may be animalistic if not utilized properly.

However, the only way to cultivate a more mindful attitude is to abandon ego and the constant urge to prove a point. If you permit your ego to continue to expand, it will ultimately absorb your conscious mind and transform you into an emotional jerk. You will begin to react rather than respond to problems when this occurs. Sigma males are, therefore, gods among men. They can contain their ego, manage negative emotions, and respond strategically to problems rather than reacting.

In a word, they respond to circumstances based on inner control. The lone wolf thinks that when one's ego is in the way, one cannot see the greater picture. Your ego will continually bring up the things you lack and how unjust the world has been to you. They may encounter a succession of disappointments, terrible experiences, and failures, but they never react to life; rather, they respond. The sigma males do not always accept their interpretations of what is occurring. This is because the mind's interpretation is based on prior experiences or insufficient information.

Nevertheless, sigma males propel life from the inside. Therefore, it is simple for them to regulate their emotions. It provides sigma males with strong self-confidence, self-respect, and self-love. No matter how unattractive or poor a sigma male is, he will always be adored. And this is because lone wolves have a way of identifying with their inner selves, awakening to their reality, and constructing it appropriately. With this, sigma males will always be in control of their emotions, regardless of the circumstances.

Key Takeaways

- Sigma males are enigmas. The more you attempt to understand them, the more you become confused. However, they cannot be ignored in a team or environment. People listen anytime they talk, and their wishes are granted when they ask.

- Sigma males have matured that what to say during a conversation comes effortlessly. They always know what to say in any given circumstance.

- By speaking less, sigma males subconsciously impress and frighten others. Since lone wolves comprehend the human mind, they know that the more they speak, the more foolish they would appear.

- Whatever the sigma males say, they carefully consider it before uttering it. The lone wolves are incredibly cautious with their words to avoid uttering anything they would later regret.

- Sigma males have a great level of emotional control. Regardless of their emotions, they do not respond to difficulties with naivety.

- Establishing healthy boundaries is a behavior that makes sigma males mentally strong. Regardless of your relationship with the sigma male, he will always set his limits.

- Sigma males always accept responsibility. Regardless of what occurred, they do not hold anyone accountable.

- The lone wolves are life-realistic, knowing that not everything is perfect and that things do not always go as planned. Sigma males view setbacks and obstacles as components of what makes life exciting.

Dear Reader,

As independent authors it's often difficult to gather reviews compared with much bigger publishers.

Therefore, please leave a review on the platform where you bought this book.

Many thanks,

Author Team

CHAPTER 5

SIGMA MALE PERSONALITY

Why Sigma Males Have a High Level of Self Awareness

The fact that sigma males possess a high self-awareness distinguishes them in the manosphere. They regularly monitor their self-concept and ideas. And because sigma males are continuously conscious of their current conditions, they always possess a high level of self-awareness. They aspire to be better versions of themselves than they were yesterday. Even if the activities of sigma males are not motivated by money, they have a distinct view of wealth. They desire riches, and they shape their mentality accordingly. You will never find a sigma male who secretly despises the wealthy. The lone wolves believe that subconsciously loathing affluent people might hinder one's journey to a successful future.

In a word, sigma males think that anything you despise in your head will eventually result in your own shortcomings. Your success in life is contingent upon how well you comprehend your self-concept. The greater your self-awareness, the greater your chances of achieving success.

Males in the beta and omega subgroups lack self-awareness. These individuals live on autopilot and expect everything to fall into place. This explains why Beta and Omega males do not change unless they undergo a traumatic event. Pain can cause intelligent Beta and Omega males to introspect and search for their inner monsters. When Beta or Omega males endure this traumatic event, they will go on a path of self-discovery. And a few of them may become improved versions of themselves or even sigma males.

On the other hand, high-level sigma males do not wait for great discomfort before improving themselves. The lone wolves are continually transforming. People frequently look on the bright side when confronted with difficult circumstances or adversity. Sigma males never view themselves as failures or undeserving of being successful, regardless of the circumstances. The lone wolf believes in the law of attraction. Hence they attempt to remain optimistic in any circumstances, which explains why they are consistently successful in most of their endeavors. They think self-perception dictates your life experiences and how others regard you. For example, if you claim to be broke, you will continue to endure financial hardship regardless of your income. But if you adjust your perspective and begin finding the good in everything, you will experience optimism. The sigma males think that whatever your current circumstances, the situation will eventually improve if you choose the road of positivity. Although, at first, it may appear that you are deceiving yourself, with perseverance, you will begin to experience optimism in all parts of your life. The lone wolf believes that God is within every man. And the manifestation of this divinity in your life results from the guidance you provide it. For example, there is no distinction between affluent and poor men.

While the wealthy individual constantly feels he is rich and works diligently to attain wealth. The poor man's perception that he is impoverished will deter him from making an effort necessary to achieve his goals. In reality, nothing changes in the world of sigma males until they know it. They constantly listen to all the voices in their head, both excellent and negative, and eliminate the negative ones while enhancing the positive ones. The fact is that reality is a mirror that always reflects your innermost ideas. And you cannot alter your reality until you alter your thinking. Now you see why the lives of sigma males usually appear so fantastic. Sigma males think that every man is an actor portraying many roles. And the role you choose to play can ultimately influence the course of your life. Every man, according to the sigma males, is boundless. They can do and possess anything and only require the proper mentality.

How Others See Sigma Males

The sigma male enjoys going outside the norm. Rules are intended to be broken or, at the very least, bypassed. Sigma males refuse to be constrained by tradition and others' expectations. They are impervious to the pressures and expectations of society and are unconcerned with how a particular behavior may impact their social idea. Sigma males disbelieve in society's established hierarchical systems. They position themselves outside conventional authority structures, making it practically hard to direct them. They instead follow their internal moral compass.

The Sigma Male Can Be Intimidating at Work

One thing is sure: a sigma male will never sit in a cubicle and accept instructions from a manager! Sigma males like to be their authority in the workplace. They are business owners, digital nomads, freelancers, innovators, creatives, or occupy one of the company's top roles. They do however, recognize that others are required to accomplish specific objectives.

They Are Incredibly Confident

While alpha males are recognized for their outward confidence, sigma males are known for their introverted confidence. At first glance, they may not appear to be the most assertive individuals in the room. A sigma male does not need to demonstrate authority to feel better. The source of his self-esteem is not social media, other people's opinions, or approbation. They are sure of who they are and fully understand what they enjoy and dislike.

Adventurous and Nomadic

Sigma males do not comply with conventional career norms and trajectories and like to take the road less traveled and figure out life as they go. Curiosity-driven, he enjoys going on excursions and searching out new experiences. Instead of remaining in his comfort zone, the sigma male seeks out new cultures, tastes, and people. These unique experiences invigorate him. He tests his limitations and explores new vistas, drawing strength from the unknown. This does not imply that they act irresponsibly since they carefully consider their actions.

They Have Heightened Awareness of Their Environment

Sigma males are exceedingly self-aware, and their hours of seclusion frequently result in reflection. He often considers his behaviors and knows how they affect his complete existence. He accurately understands his strengths and actively strives to improve his deficiencies. If he makes a mistake, he is quick to convert it into a learning experience. As a result of not having to explain their status in society, their emotions and aspirations take center stage. They are aware of their life goals and continually strive for self-improvement.

Intimidating Traits of the Sigma Males

Contrary to popular belief, sigma males are not thugs. However, they have a formidable demeanor that frequently intimidates others. Lone wolves are neither noisy, aggressive, or dominant. However, they possess scary characteristics that put others on guard. Due to their high self-confidence, sigma males are not scared to express themselves most suitably. Even standing before an authority, they will not hesitate to convey their feelings.

Sigma Males Are Opinionated and Persuasive

One characteristic that makes sigma males intimidating is their opinionated and persuasive. Unfortunately, this is sometimes misinterpreted as arrogance. The thoughts of sigma males are under their control, and others do not readily sway them. Sigma males appreciate intellectually fascinating talks and strongly believe in their opinions and principles. Despite being steadfast in their opinions and principles, sigma males constantly consider the perspectives of others. Even when someone says something unimportant, a sigma male will not demean them. And sigma males can persuade others to see things from their perspective through well-reasoned and convincing arguments. The lone wolf is dissatisfied if they cannot persuade others to see things from their perspective. In the end, they appreciate everyone's perspective and way of thinking.

Sigma Males Are Decisive

The definite nature of sigma males makes them appear scary to others. Do not misunderstand; sigma males are not impulsive while making decisions. They analyze their alternatives thoroughly but do not allow themselves to become mired in the decision-making process. The lone wolves are unlike the Alpha and Beta males, who occasionally have analytical paralysis while making judgments. In reality, sigma males constantly rely on their intellect and instinct to make the right choices. Rarely anything annoys a sigma male more than seeing others squander time deliberating over situations that may be readily solved.

According to the lone wolf, a genuine man should be courageous and take action when necessary, rather than waiting for someone else to assist them in making a decision. They are more rational than emotionally driven. The majority of sigma males are motivated by logic rather than emotion. When addressing challenges, they depend on their intellect and instincts. Males of the Sigma class do not allow personal feelings to impair their judgment. Every time they make a decision, sigma males consider the consequences of their actions.

Typically, sigma males cannot tolerate the presence of beta and omega guys. These men are so uneducated in a world filled with knowledge. And if a sigma male discovers you are ignorant and careless regarding education or requiring critical study, he will begin to avoid you.

They Do Not Allow Strangers into Their Lives

In general, sigma males are selective about the people they accept into their lives. They are aware that individuals may be inconsistent, so they take precautions before allowing new people into their lives.

The sigma males' friendship attitude is that it is preferable to be alone and authentic than surrounded by phony people. Sigma males do not require the approval of others to develop confidence, and they dot all the I's and cross all the T's before letting anyone into their lives. The sigma males' friendship attitude is that it is preferable to be alone and authentic than surrounded by phony people.

They Do Not Require the Approval of Others

The lone wolves are aware of their identities and capabilities; therefore, they don't care what people think of them. Even if the sigma male has yet to determine who he is, he does not require anyone's approval to know what he is capable of. Despite their life challenges, sigma males will ultimately discover who they are. Therefore, lone wolves have a limited group of friends with whom they are always content. Regarding friendship, sigma males prefer to have a few loyal and trustworthy friends over many somewhat constant social circles.

They Never Deviate from Their Values

One of the terrifying characteristics of sigma males is that they consistently adhere to their values. Every sigma male understands what he stands for, and they never compromise his ideals and values. Once something doesn't seem right, it is impossible to convince a sigma male to participate. And the activities of lone wolves define the actions they deem acceptable and unacceptable in others. Whether you are the sigma male's boss or the most dreaded tyrant, he informs you with confidence if you fall out of line.

Sigma Males Do Not Seek Attention

Sigma males do not seek attention, and they require personal space. However, their remarkable nature draws others to them constantly. Sigma males are not like Beta and Omega males, who would do everything to gain the attention of others. It's amusing how people are instinctively drawn to sigma males despite their attempts to blend in. Perhaps this is because lone wolves want the welfare of others. Interestingly, sigma males' socialization is not directly motivated by them. But by those who are influenced by the lone wolf's distinctive characteristics.

Sigma Males Do Not Live to Please Others

Sigma males do not live for the sake of impressing or pleasing others. They have no fear of being themselves. The lone wolf does not care if they cause a few feathers to be ruffled; they will always be themselves. What would you expect from a personality such as the sigma males? They have confidence and self-assurance. Sigma males never need to go out of their way to please or impress others, regardless of the circumstances. Even though sigma males are dedicated to achieving success, they do not do it at the sacrifice of their self-respect. The lone wolves never conceal their actual nature and are unrepentant for their acts.

Sigma Males Are Goal Oriented

Sigma males are goal-oriented and consistently focus on a specific goal and devise strategies to realize it. The sigma males have constant clarity of ideas. And they do not doubt or believe that their dreams are unrealistic. It does not matter what obstacles they face. The lone wolves are aware of the actions necessary to attain their goals. They are laser-focused on completing their smaller and more defined goals to reach their long-term objectives.

Sigma Males Will Not Accept Excuses

Sigma males despise the use of excuses as a replacement for effort. It disgusts sigma males when individuals complain about their inability to adequately manage their time and then find an external cause to blame for their inefficiency. The lone wolf always focuses on what they can do and find strategies to overcome hurdles. Once a sigma male has made up his mind to overcome an obstacle, he will always do so, regardless of its size.

Ways Sigma Males Assess People's Confidence

The sigma males feel that self-assurance is the most attractive quality a person may possess. They think that confidence is more advantageous than wealth and fear. Due to the confidence of the lone wolf, everyone else believes they cannot compete with them. And that gives them an advantage every time. When you feel most confident, you will always discover your God-given abilities and natural talents. Sigma males are aware that insecurity is contagious. Therefore, they associate more with bold and incredibly confident individuals.

This section will describe how sigma males evaluate the confidence of others. Before developing a deep relationship with someone, sigma males typically evaluate their confidence level. Moreover, sigma males observe an increasing number of individuals with low or nonexistent confidence. Failing the confidence test for sigma males is not the end; however, you may miss a tremendous chance. Regardless of the sort of connection the sigma male wishes to engage with you, he will first inquire about your degree of confidence. You cannot become the sigma male's business partner, for instance, if you are as timid as a rabbit. Insecure individuals are less likely to succeed in any activity. Behind the fight of worries, there are typically countless unrealized chances. And if you cannot emancipate yourself from this shackle of dread, your professional and personal life will not progress. People with little possibility for growth cannot be friends with lone wolves.

Accepting Responsibility for Actions

One of the easiest ways to identify persons who lack confidence is when they refuse to accept responsibility for their actions. These individuals fear taking responsibility for their acts because they are too worried about what others think of them. These individuals have probably endured traumatic events such as criticism, painful maltreatment, rejection, and betrayal. As a result, they lack self-assurance and cannot accept responsibility for their acts. They find a way to criticize the system or their coworkers whenever they commit an error. The sigma male will quickly recognize your lack of self-confidence upon observing this feature.

Defensive Posture

Your body language can convey self-assurance to a sensitive personality, such as the sigma male. Every action you do reveals a great deal about your character. The sigma males can determine if you are confident, trustworthy, or afraid by a gesture. Therefore, you lack self-confidence if you always adopt protective bodily postures such as folding your hands or crossing your knees when speaking.

Avoiding Eye Contact

Eye contact is one of the most crucial nonverbal indicators used by sigma males to evaluate the self-confidence, self-esteem, and assertiveness of others. When you glance down or about during a discussion, you convey the appearance that you are tense. While chatting, if you cannot keep eye contact with the sigma male, he will instantly recognize that you lack confidence. A sigma male would find it quite challenging to conduct business with someone who has lost self-confidence or self-esteem. 60 to 70 percent eye contact during a discussion helps you connect with the other person. According to the Idiap Research Institute research, eye contact indicates social rank and authority in the discussion.

Reaction to Stressful Situations

Your behavior in a difficult circumstance may reveal a great deal about your character and self-confidence. People typically lose their composure in stressful situations. If you lack self-confidence or have poor self-esteem, you tend to be quickly irritated, confused, upset, and irritable. People who lack self-confidence are perpetually oblivious to challenging situations, and it will be tough for them to relax and clear their minds to generate new solutions. Therefore, if a sigma male notices that you feel horrible about yourself, lonely, useless, or unhappy, he will automatically conclude that you lack self-confidence.

How Sigma Males Develop Their Superpowers (Sigma Male Subconscious Mind)

Sigma males possess a great degree of self-awareness. They recognize that every man is a sleeping titan with unfathomable potential. However, most individuals do not know how to access these potentials since they do not comprehend how the subconscious mind operates. To a sigma male, everyone possesses a secret skill. And if you discover your unique and innate talent, you will have an advantage over most individuals. Due to their self-awareness, the sigma males can cultivate their abilities intentionally. This explains why they appear always to be ahead of everyone.

This section explains how sigma males get their superpowers. All the information sigma males require to realize their unfathomable potential is hidden in their subconscious minds. This portion of their brain stores every ability, experience, memory, and belief they've ever had. Lone wolves are aware that their conscious mind is only a filter or net that captures any unwanted information before it reaches the subconscious mind. It is rather amusing that most people are unaware that their subconscious thoughts influence around 99 percent of their actions. However, because sigma males have high self-awareness, they are aware of this and pay close attention to their subconscious brains.

They know you may adopt the incorrect mentality and viewpoint if you ignore your subconscious mind. Once your subconscious has been programmed along this route, it becomes difficult to alter your behavior. And this will eventually influence how you perceive yourself and others around you. Your beliefs shape who you are and are strongly connected to your subconscious mind. Intriguingly, they have mental control because sigma males comprehend their subconscious mind and how to train it. This will eventually aid in the development of their abilities. It is rather amusing that most males in the manosphere are unaware of the existence of the subconscious mind, much less how to train and control it.

The fact that sigma males comprehend how the subconscious mind functions place them ahead of all other men. Sigma males know that every feeling they encounter originates in the subconscious and controls their respiration and other bodily processes. They are aware that their acts every second of every day train their subconscious mind directly or indirectly. This explains why sigma males are always mindful of their actions and how they handle circumstances. For instance, whenever you panic in a stressful situation, you train your subconscious to handle such situations.

Each fault and strength in a sigma male's personality result from learned behavior. Their internal sentiments, emotions, and other phenomena result from programming in their subconscious mind. However, lone wolves have power over their subconscious; they may rapidly unlearn a behavior or form a new routine. The fact that sigma males understand how their subconscious mind functions make it easier for them to tap into their unfathomable potential. It enables sigma males to influence others and persuade them to perceive things from their perspective. They bypass these individuals' conscious brains and speak directly to their unconscious minds.

After reading this book, you will realize why sigma males are gods among men. Sigma males are masters of persuasion and have the ability to exert a strong influence on others because they comprehend the rule guiding the human subconscious mind. So, these are the subconscious mind's laws and the sigma males employ to obtain actual superpowers.

Distinguishing Between Real and Fake

Most of the time, the subconscious mind cannot distinguish between what is real and what is not. What you feed your subconscious mind will determine what it programs. Similar to a computer program, you receive what you provide. Have you ever considered how your brain reacts when you think something frightening? Regardless of the integrity of your beliefs, your subconscious mind will automatically teach your brain to agree with them. The sigma males are aware of this rule. Therefore, they are wary of what enters their conscious mind. Your subconscious mind is programmed with whatever you feed your conscious mind to develop your habits and behavior. Even though the sigma male has some reckless ideas in their conscious mind, they filter such thoughts and reformat their thinking to be more positive when alone. This explains why sigma males are usually optimistic in every circumstance. Regardless of what occurred or the difficulties, he is more concerned with finding a solution than panicking.

Beliefs

Our lives generally center on our beliefs. Sadly, the majority of individuals do not recognize this truth. However, because they are self-aware, sigma males recognize the significance of beliefs in their life. They are aware that their conscious minds are guided by their beliefs. People with low self-esteem feel insufficient and that everyone else is superior. And once your subconscious mind assimilates these ideas, they form the foundation of your default personality. The longer you maintain a specific belief, the harder it is to alter it. The sigma males are aware that most of our beliefs are formed throughout childhood. When left unchanged over time, these beliefs grow stronger. And these children will mature into either Beta, Omega, or Alpha males.

Every sigma male knows that beliefs are embedded in the subconscious mind like seeds. The longer they are allowed to remain, the more time they have to develop roots and spread. Do not misunderstand; it is essential to have beliefs. However, try to replace negative ideas with positive ones at all times. It distinguishes sigma males from all other men in the manosphere.

Thought Generates Physical Response

Sigma males comprehend the power of the mind and are aware that these ideas produce physical responses. This explains why lone wolves love spending time alone and contemplating their environment. This is how they replenish their creative energy, reprogram their subconscious mind, and cultivate a fresh, optimistic outlook on life.

You Receive What You Anticipate

The rule of expectancies is one of the laws that aid in developing superpowers in sigma males. The law of expectation argues that you receive just what you anticipate from life. You will achieve such outcomes if you anticipate success, confidence, and goal realization. Similarly, if you anticipate failure, you will experience it. The sigma males know this rule; they anticipate a favorable conclusion from every difficult circumstance. Regardless of how difficult a situation may appear, sigma males never cease to see the bright side.

Having a Glimmer of Hope at The End of the Tunnel

Your subconscious mind will activate the incredible superpower inside you to make your expectations a reality, regardless of your aspirations. These four subconscious mind rules assist sigma males in unlocking their limitless potential.

Toxic Things Sigma Males Never Say to Their Kids

This may come as a surprise, but sigma males may be the most incredible parents. They go above and beyond to make their children feel loved and educate them on dealing with the world's cruel realities. The lone wolves know that youngsters have delicate emotions and are highly sensitive, so they are incredibly cautious around their children. No matter how upset sigma males are, there are certain things they must never say to their children. This is because sigma males comprehend the potency of words and how they might negatively affect a youngster. Saying thoughtless words to children may create lasting impressions and memories. Sigma males comprehend the psychology of children. And they know that unpleasant comments from parents can cause significant psychological and emotional harm to them.

Offensive Words Regarding Their Appearance

No matter what occurs, sigma males never use foul language with their children. They will never use derogatory terms such as you are too short, too thin, or have horrible hair with their children. No matter how a youngster seems, sigma males will never insult a child based on appearance. They think that every child has potential. Children who undergo this degraded growth will have physical insecurity and body image concerns. And this might lead to low self-esteem and other major mental problems, such as eating disorders. The sigma males educate their children to embrace themselves regardless of physical appearance.

Action-Oriented Provocative Queries

When asked to children, some questions subconsciously influence their self-perception. For example, it is inappropriate to ask children, "Why do you act so strangely?" or "Why do you eat, move, or speak this way?" The fact is that youngsters always believe their parents' statements. Sigma males are aware of this, so they refrain from asking or making critical remarks to their children. Otherwise, these children would believe that there is something wrong with them. When children begin to believe this about themselves, it will be difficult to be themselves in social situations. And this habit might persist until maturity. Because of the few harmful things their parents say, they will continually live with the anxiety and discomfort that other people will laugh at them.

Selfish Desires

Regardless of what a youngster has done, sigma males will never express self-centered desires before that child. When a youngster hears phrases such as "I wish you had never been born," "I wish your mother had an abortion," "I regret having you," "I wish you were a different child," etc., they feel as if they were never meant to exist in this world. Sigma males are aware of the sensitivity and toxicity of these comments, and they never use them with their children. When parents use these toxic words on their children, it reduces their sense of self and may lead to depression. Most fathers never tire of making their children feel loved and cherished.

Making a Child Experience Being a Burden

Sigma males are too fond of their children to make them feel like a burden. No matter how much they spend on their children, lone wolves never make their children feel like a burden. Sigma males are not like Beta and Omega males who say harsh things to their children, such as "it's so difficult to take care of you," "you exhaust me," etc. These remarks are damaging. And addressing a child with them makes him feel like a burden. The child will begin to conceal his wants, emotions, and issues.

Sigma males do not want this for their children, so they ensure they constantly feel loved and cherished.

Inappropriate Comparisons

Unhealthy comparisons are harmful activities that sigma males never engage in with their children. Due to their sensitivity, lone wolves would never compare a youngster to their siblings, relatives, or other children, and they recognize that each child is distinct and treat them accordingly.

Phrases High-Value Sigma Males Don't Use

Lone wolves are susceptible, rational, and mature when interacting with others. Sigma males are very aware of their responses to various events and surroundings, and they have an entirely different outlook on life and see the bright side of everything.

Let's go through the five phrases and words that high-value sigma males never use.

But I Don't Feel Like It

Sigma males are constantly mindful of their words. Because they are perceptive, they comprehend the subtext of every statement you make. People frequently use this expression when they do not want to complete necessary tasks, suggesting that these individuals ignore their responsibilities. And if it occurs in the workplace, it will not make a favorable impression on your employer or direct supervisor.

You might become bored or exhausted with the work at hand. But it is usually preferable to do these jobs promptly so that you may focus on other tasks.

Shut Up!

One of the expressions that high-value sigma males refrain from using is "Shut Up!" They would prefer an intellectually engaging or sensible discourse to one that is emotional. The phrase "shut up" during a discussion suggests a lack of emotional development. If the sigma male is irritated by the conversation, he would prefer to use a remark such as "could you just be quiet?" or casually walk away. As previously indicated, sigma males are constantly in charge of their emotions. Therefore, irrespective of how angry they may be, lone wolves never shout "shut up." It is both insulting and weakens the sigma male's appearance.

You Are Not My Mother

In general, sigma males dislike dealing with someone who is very controlling or authoritative. However, kids will not say, "you are not my mother." When sigma males want to address someone's domineering or dictatorial conduct, they will do it without using this expression. For instance, if you sound excessively domineering or dictatorial, the lone wolf will express displeasure with your actions. However, he will not compare you to his parents or use other unpleasant terms

Whatever

Someone with the sensitivity of a sigma male would never utter the term whatever. It is not cool and disregards what has been stated in a conversation. It is a term frequently employed by emotionally immature individuals. They utilize this statement instead of acknowledging their error or apologizing for their behavior. This expression gives the impression that you are immature and lack self-confidence

Why Can't You Do it

"Why can't you do it?" is one of the high-value questions that sigma males avoid asking. This remark conveys the idea that you are lazy and often avoid work

Types of Attraction the Sigma Males Experience

Attraction is interpreted differently by sigma males, extending beyond romantic or sexual attraction to a person. The attraction has a crucial influence on how sigma males interact with other individuals. For instance, sigma males may appreciate someone due to their intelligence but do not seek a romantic connection with her.

Similarly, a sigma male may desire a romantic connection, but he does not feel the need to be intimate. And because sigma males comprehend their attraction to individuals, they rarely experience emotional confusion.

Romantic Attraction

Sigma males sense romantic desire when they discover the appropriate lady for a love connection. When a sigma male feels romantically attracted to someone, he may desire to be with that person regardless of the sexual component.

Sexual Attraction

Sexual attraction is one kind of attraction experienced by sigma males. It causes lone wolves to seek sexual interaction or develop sexual desires for another individual. This attraction evokes feelings of passion, desire, or affection in the sigma male.

Physical Attraction

Physical attraction, often known as sensuous attraction, is the urge of a sigma male to be near someone he trusts and cares about. Despite their preference for seclusion, sigma males nevertheless want to be physically cared for and treated with love and compassion by someone near their hearts.

Nevertheless, physical attraction is not always the only factor; other forms of attraction sometimes accompany it. When sigma males sense a physical attraction, they yearn to be touched or handled by a close companion. However, it may not be a sexual or romantic touch, and it might be expressed through hugs or kisses.

Aesthetic Attraction

Aesthetic attraction is an attraction exhibited by sigma males towards attractive individuals. The sigma males will admire these people's attractiveness but will not care about them. If you deeply understand sigma males, you will realize that they appreciate beauty. Again, a sigma male's appreciation of a person's appearance does not necessarily indicate romantic interest.

Psychological Attraction

Generally speaking, sigma males are more logical than emotive. However, they still possess feelings; they are, after all, human. There are times when lone wolves need emotional proximity with another individual, and Sigma males might experience emotional attraction to their acquaintances, relatives, love partners, etc.

Occasionally, lone wolves may desire to connect emotionally with the significant individuals in their lives. When this does occur, the sigma males may discuss their opinions and feelings about a specific topic and, more crucially, their experiences.

Intellectual Attraction

Intellectual attraction is the most prevalent attraction experienced by sigma males, who desire to engage with others on a higher intellectual level. Sapiosexuality is an additional term for the intellectual attraction (the tendency to attract highly intelligent people). If you frequently engage sigma males in highly intelligent discourse, it will be simpler for them to connect with you.

When a person is insightful, thoughtful, and exhibits a high IQ during a discussion, sigma males find them extremely appealing. This type of attraction is referred to as the intellectual attraction of sapiosexuality. And sigma males find it difficult to be emotionally or physically attracted to someone who cannot cognitively fulfill them.

Silly Questions Sigma Males Don't Ask

Usually, it is simple to determine a person's intelligence and thoughtfulness based on their questions. Sigma males are aware of this, so they are constantly mindful of the questions they ask in a given context.

Never will the lone wolf ask an embarrassing or unnecessary question. Sigma males have a high level of self-awareness; therefore, they do not speak before they think. Instead, they engage in creative thought before speaking.

This part will provide the five questions that sigma males never ask. It is simple to identify the beta and omega males in a group. Do you realize why? They consistently ask questions that make them look ignorant and unimaginative. These individuals only seek to impress others without regard for what they say. Therefore, sigma males consistently outperform them in every circumstance. Although sigma males are not competing with omega, beta, or alpha males, their thinking and perceptive nature make them the focal point of any group. Similar to goldfish in a dish. Remember that the goldfish have nowhere to hide.

Don't You Think We Should?

Do you not agree that we ought to do this instead of that? Alternatively, don't you believe we should go to store A instead of B? Sigma males never ask such questions. Do you realize why? This is because these sorts of queries are closed-ended and do not allow for the participation of other individuals. It's a method of presuming your concept is flawless and wanting everyone else to concur and nod in agreement. Because sigma males are intelligent and wise, they comprehend the ramifications of such concerns. Therefore, they never ask questions in this manner. They prefer to pose their questions so that others may discuss, participate, and generate potential solutions to an issue.

Why Aren't You?

This is another inquiry type that sigma males do not ask—asking someone why they are not enrolled in college. Why don't you have a significant other? Why are you not reading, etc., raises many questions?

They cause the recipient to feel uneasy, insulted, and occasionally defensive. Sigma males comprehend human behavior from a psychological standpoint. They know that asking such questions makes others feel like they are not on the same timeline as everyone else. Moreover, these inquiries are frequently perceived as critical, condescending, and disrespectful. Males of the Sigma class recognize that people are unique and tend to behave differently. They are aware that individuals have diverse origins and circumstances. Therefore, it is normal that they have varied timelines. Consequently, it is inappropriate and judgmental to ask someone such questions.

Why Do You Look Like This?

Typically, sigma males are highly sensitive and empathic. And they will never inquire about a person's physical appearance.

The lone wolf doesn't care if someone is overweight, unattractive, have large eyes, etc. And they will never inquire as to why they seem as they do. They know that discussing a person's physical appearance is a delicate subject. Questions and remarks on a person's looks are inappropriate and can cause the individual to feel bad about themselves.

It makes no difference if your intentions are sincere or whether you care about their well-being. Such questions are delicate, and in reality, you have no idea what they are experiencing. And asking them delicate questions about their looks may make matters worse.

What Can I Give This Individual?

People frequently ask themselves this when they like someone. These are questions that Sigma males never ask themselves because they induce self-doubt. It causes a person to question if they are worthy of friendship or romantic affection. Therefore, when sigma males like someone, they do not consider what to present them as much, and they follow their inclinations and offer the recipient any present they choose.

The lone wolf recognizes that friendship and relationships are not comparable to contracts, and you are not required to calculate what you give and receive from one another. You do not need to consider how to get someone's attention or affection. Sigma males recognize that being in a relationship or friendship with someone transcends career, appearance, and even financial status. What truly matters are your unique characteristics and eccentricities; these constitute your personality. Once you are yourself in the presence of others, they will undoubtedly adore and respect you for who you are.

Should You Not Know My Needs and Wants?

This is the most idiotic question imaginable, and this question makes no sense regardless of whether the individual is your buddy or your lover. Even if you have known someone for a long time, you cannot assume that they are aware of your needs and desires. Sigma males know this reality and do not pose such an idiotic question. Sigma males prefer to disclose their wants rather than assume that others already know them.

Key Takeaways

- Sigma males think that anything you despise so much in your head will always be far away. Your success in life is contingent upon how well you comprehend your self-concept. The greater your confidence, the greater your chances of achieving success.

- Sigma males refuse to be constrained by tradition and others' expectations. They are impervious to the pressures and expectations of society and are unconcerned with how a particular behavior may impact their social idea.

- Sigma males are exceedingly self-aware, and their hours of seclusion frequently result in reflection.

- According to the lone wolf, a genuine man should be courageous and take action when necessary, rather than waiting for someone else to assist them in making a decision.

- The fact that sigma males comprehend how the subconscious mind functions place them ahead of all other men. Sigma males know that every feeling they encounter originates in the subconscious and controls their respiration and other bodily processes.

- Every sigma male knows that beliefs are embedded in the subconscious mind like seeds. The longer they are allowed to remain, the more time they have to develop roots and spread.

- A sigma male may desire a romantic relationship, but he does not feel the need to be intimate. And because sigma males comprehend their attraction to individuals, they rarely experience emotional confusion.

CHAPTER 6

SIGMA MALE DATING STRATEGIES

Ways Women Secretly Test the Sigma Males

Wherever they go, sigma males constantly emanate an atmosphere of secrecy and evasion. This makes it challenging for women to comprehend and anticipate their future actions. Even though they appear mysterious, women find sigma males extremely appealing. Once a woman develops a crush on a lone wolf, she would test him to determine whether he possesses the qualities she values in a spouse. She would want to know the sigma male's attentiveness, concentration, and selflessness.

Remember that sigma males are indifferent to what others think of them. Even if they fail these examinations, it is of little concern to them. However, as time passes, you tend to become less of a Sigma Male, as true Sigma Males will always pass these tests.

They Assess the Masculinity of Sigma Males

Typically, women test a sigma male to determine his strength, and having well-developed muscles does not indicate strength. This is not the sort of strength that women want. The majority of women desire a man with a masculine appearance. But ladies like to be with a man with mental and emotional power and physical strength. When a woman evaluates a sigma male, she evaluates his emotional strength. Once a woman discovers that a sigma male possesses emotional strength comparable to steel's, she will naturally fall in love with him. Believe me, gentlemen, no woman wants to be with an insecure, psychologically unstable, or insane man. They require a partner who is composed, emotionally developed, and focused.

And typically, sigma males always possess these characteristics. Guys! No lady with a serious disposition would date a Beta or Omega male. Some of these men frequently portray themselves as Sigma males. They will fake their strengths until they win the lady's heart, at which point they will unveil themselves. Women are aware of these individuals; thus, they must check for mental and emotional maturity before dating any male.

They Evaluate the Sigma Males' Self-Assurance

Women evaluate sigma males to determine if they are as confident as they look. Every sigma male of high worth has great self-assurance and emotional strength, and these two characteristics make the sigma male look scary to others. You may ask why women want to test the confidence of sigma males. However, you cannot fault them. Several men give off the appearance that they are pretty confident. However, you will discover that they are as self-doubting and afraid as a rabbit when placed in a challenging circumstance.

They Determine Whether the Man Cares for Them

Typically, women want to know if a man cares about them enough to commit to a long-term relationship. Men uninterested in a woman will make it apparent that she will not spend her time with them. Sigma males are not like Beta or Omega males who pretend to care in order to get what is between their legs. Therefore, most women would like to know whether a sigma male is interested in a short-term relationship or a long-term commitment.

But are you aware of the irony? Women are attracted to males who are less interested in them. It's pretty contradictory, yet it's the truth. Why would a woman pursue a man with no interest in her? It all boils down to the reality that women enjoy mysteries. And the more mysterious a man appears to them, the more appealing he will be. Women are aware that men who are less interested in them are always the most desirable partners.

This explains why even when a sigma male makes it apparent he is not interested in a woman; she continues to pursue him. Yes, women will always desire the impossible. However, she will view you as desperate once you demonstrate an interest in her. And she will attempt to be elusive.

They Want to Determine if The Sigma Males Are Real or Not

Authenticity is one area in which women covertly evaluate sigma males. We are in a world rife with lies. Not always are things as they appear. Every action will always be motivated by ulterior considerations. There are so many phony men in the world, and they are only being polite to a woman to seduce her. My point? In life, people may be deceiving. And some of history's most wicked men could sustain their evil crimes through deceit. Some men (particularly Beta and Omega males) may exhibit different bizarre behaviors to attract women. For example, many men create the appearance that they are wealthy.

They hire expensive sports vehicles to impress others, purchase expensive beverages, and live lavish lifestyles. In actuality, though, these men may be poorer than the ordinary man who earns a respectable living and does not flaunt it. When women begin dating these men, they often discover that despite their seeming wealth, they are genuinely mired in poverty. And due to circumstances like this, women surreptitiously test men, particularly sigma males. If you know sigma males well, you would realize that they despise being fake. Once a sigma male discovers that a woman is exhibiting a fake personality, he quickly loses interest in her, regardless of her beauty and intelligence.

In a nutshell, women conduct tests on sigma males to verify who they claim to be. The more the sigma males understand women and their true motivations for testing them, the greater their ability to influence these women's conduct.

How Semen Retention Makes Sigma Males Immortal

Semen retention may sound like an outrageous new trend, yet the practice may be as old as humanity itself. It is the technique of avoiding ejaculation on purpose. You can engage in this practice by refraining from all sexual activity, halting before ejaculation, or learning to climax without ejaculating.

This section will explain how semen retention makes sigma males powerful. Every individual has two alternatives in life: becoming immortal or reproductive. Those who wish to attain immortality transform into sigma males. Thus, the gods among men. When a sigma male transforms into a retainer, he enters eternal mode since he no longer needs to discharge his life energy. Once he ceases engaging in frequent sexual activity, his body enters self-management or immortality mode. In this context, the self-management mode refers to creating more testosterone. This fills the sigma male's body with additional vitamins and minerals, healing their central nervous system, stimulating their cells and receptors such as dopamine and serotonin, thickening their hair, and unblocking their chakras, among other benefits.

The more sperm sigma males maintain, the more they will develop vigor, confidence, and masculinity. The majority of high-quality sigma males always retain their sperm, which explains why they are energetic, have lofty ambitions, and have a higher frequency. Rarely do you observe high-value sigma males squandering sperm cells. The sigma males recognize that the sperm they possess is their life energy, providing everything necessary for immortality. That is, by multiplying their cells. It helps heal damaged cells, improves brain function, boosts self-confidence, and increases the drive to commit, execute, and accomplish goals. Once you go on a semen retention adventure, you will find that semen retention has a therapeutic element that impacts you.

The lone wolves realize that being a retainer aids them in amassing power and maturing into what a man should be. You should know about semen retention because it is not a one-time occurrence but a comprehensive journey that influences your physical, mental, and spiritual well-being. Consequently, the immortality of the sigma males results from four levels of semen preservation.

Physical

This is the initial level of semen retention that sigma males must comprehend to attain immortality. Permit me to note that being a retainer is more about avoiding porn and masturbation than orgasm. Surprisingly, some individuals have less closeness with the other sex than masturbation. For these individuals, masturbation is the primary method of sperm discharge. And you cannot gain the benefits of sexual abstinence unless you conquer porn and masturbation. Porn and masturbation raise cortisol levels (the stress hormone), prolactin, dopamine, and norepinephrine. Because your neurotransmitters are oversaturated, you may experience tiredness and lack happiness.

According to a study, the generation of sperm is the body's greatest energy priority. Ancient Taoists cautioned males against frequently ejaculating, as their vital life force is lost each time they produce sperm. Sigma males are aware of this truth. Therefore, they stop from PMO (Porn and masturbation to orgasm). And this aids in the brain's dewiring, rewiring to normal states, and cessation of excessive neurotransmitter production. After becoming a retainer, you will be more concentrated and resistant to pain, possibly because the pressure to produce sperm has subsided. It allows you to free up your body's inherent energy resources so they may be used to repair other places. Over time, you will acquire a deeper voice, thicker hair, and a more defined jawline. After a month of pure retention, you may start to feel physically better depending on the volume of semen you release every day. However, it takes about six months to begin noticing more impressive results.

Mental

The mental effects of masturbation and pornography are also present. Because sigma males are aware of this, they avoid it. These acts may cause your brain to weaken and become more dramatic. When this occurs, you will acquire a heightened libido, brain fog, a lack of motivation, sadness, and anxiety, among other symptoms. Being a retainer provides mental tranquility and gives you a new outlook on life. You will begin to perceive mundane, acceptable, and even delightful things. You now get why sigma males are constantly at their peak performance. Semen retention enables sigma males to continue throughout their lives and experience experiences that most individuals lose out on. Men who ejaculate too frequently typically experience diminished attention and elevated anxiety.

Emotional

The act of releasing sperm frequently hinders one's psychological development. Young individuals may acquire PMO addiction as a means of coping with adversity. However, it develops an addiction with time. And when this occurs, it freezes the brain and hinders their psychological development. People who ejaculate regularly behave psychologically like children.

They are devoid of male purpose, and they cannot even establish limits. Now you see why Beta and Omega guys are frequently immature in their outlook on life. However, because most high-value sigma males are retainers, their acts are more mature. They have a more sophisticated outlook, have higher expectations of women and life, and do not live in a dream world of quick satisfaction. Once you become a retainer, the kid within you will go, and the man within you will emerge.

Spiritual

It is common knowledge that the spiritual realm is immaterial. However, it is the most crucial step in the sigma male semen retention trip to immortality. The sin of desire influences your entire spiritual environment, impacting your connection with God, other creatures, and the planet itself. Sigma males can enjoy the world to its fullest because they retain sperm, which aids them in seeing people and things as they are. Maintain your vitality, and you will be surprised by how confident and powerful you become.

How Sigma Males Associate With Women

Sigma males may be cryptic, mysterious, and prefer being alone. However, they wish to avoid conflict with women for whatever reason. Irrespective of the circumstances, sigma males will never dispute or fight with a woman. Surprisingly, when they find the proper lady who understands them, they fall madly in love with her.

Women are consistently drawn to sigma males. They pursue the lone wolf and attempt to comprehend him. However, the more they attempt to comprehend the sigma male, the more complex and mysterious he gets. In contrast to alpha, omega, and beta males, it is tough for women to divert or sway sigma males to see things from their perspective. When a sigma male is in the presence of a woman, he anticipates her every action and is aware of what she will do next.

They Drive Women To Be Better

Unlike other guys, lone wolves do not tell women what they want to hear. Regardless of how it may affect a woman's emotions, sigma males will tell them the truth. Due to their life experiences, they speak to any lady confidently and without regard for her reaction. Sigma males comprehend the superpower of women and will use it against them. Therefore, it is simple for sigma males to drive a woman to be better. They do the action exquisitely. They first determine the woman's superpower and then utilize it to manipulate her.

Sigma Males Are Utterly Unpredictable

There is no way you can foresee the actions of sigma males. When they are near women, they speak less, making it impossible to predict the following action of sigma males. Typically, while in the company of women, alpha and beta males talk excessively about themselves. And this makes them highly accessible to women. When a woman is near a sigma male, he attempts to comprehend his behavior in various situations. Sometimes, they purposefully do measures to gauge the response of the sigma males. Even when a lady attempts to entice a sigma male, he keeps his focus and attitude.

Sigma Males Dislike Being Told What to Do

One of the qualities women appreciate most in sigma males is that they dislike being told what to do. They have their thinking and make judgments without hesitation. Sigma males would instead make errors and learn from them than be given orders.

Women who have previously dated Alpha, Beta, or omega guys will find sigma males so enigmatic and elusive. Sigma males cannot be told what to do, and they enjoys life on their terms and moves to the rhythm of their drum. Because sigma males are unpredictable and dislike being told what to do, it is difficult for a woman to influence or control them.

Sigma Males Are Extremely Straightforward

Sigma males are not hypocritical. They are simple and avoid obscuring their intention. A typical woman wants a man to apologize to her and confess he was wrong—most women like this. Some women may date guys who are likely to fail to gain the upper hand in the relationship. However, sigma males are uncomplicated. They always tell their partners the truth and never provide an apology for what has occurred. And this is because they do not spend their life to impress anyone, not even women.

Sigma Males Do Not Overthink Matters

Sigma males never overthink situations. They live life on their terms and follow their path. Therefore, if things are not planned, sigma males always have a backup plan. And if plan B fails, they have more options, more options, and more options. In reality, sigma males will instead develop alternative solutions to an issue than overthinking the situation. After all, excessive thought never resolves an issue. The lone wolf has a backup strategy for all of his actions. Therefore, he has no cause to be worried if things do not go according to plan; all he must do is activate the next plan of action.

In this regard, though, beta guys perform poorly. Essentially, they wish to cover every area of life. And they ultimately become inferior versions of themselves. At all times, beta guys are concerned with their appearance, demeanor, friendliness, gentleness, etc. They spend their entire lives attempting to impress others. However, sigma males live with the understanding that life is imperfect. Therefore, he has no incentive to overanalyze the situation if things do not go his way. All he must do is implement an alternative course of action.

Consequently, they are consistently successful in all their activities. They dare to tackle life head-on. Even in challenging circumstances, they strive to make the best of it.

Sigma Males Are Always in Charge of Their Sexual Life

Sigma males are constantly in control of their sexual lives, making them unpredictable to women. As their lone superpower, women are sometimes so enamored with sigma males that they fling themselves sexually at them. However, as I noted previously, seduction is generally ineffective with sigma males. He will not mount a lady simply because she seduces him. In fact, the more a sigma male is seduced, the more reasons he has to avoid you. However, the greatest approach to attracting a sigma male's attention is for a woman to be intelligent, driven, and ambitious.

Sigma Males Do Not Seek the Advice of Others

Sigma males are excellent researchers. They have such faith in the effectiveness of research. They would prefer to spend time investigating an idea or learning more about a topic than asking another person for clarification. Sigma males have solutions to their lifetime questions. He would use the Internet, read books, and other methods to get knowledge. But ultimately, he will always find what he seeks. Indeed, they feel comfortable in isolation, and time spent alone enables them to become outstanding researchers. Women do not feel intelligent when around sigma males because lone wolves have limited knowledge of everything. He is a voracious researcher and has access to a wealth of material.

With these characteristics, it is simple for sigma males to control women.

Red Flags Sigma Males Never Overlook in a Woman

Sigma males are logical in all aspects of life, and therefore, they always have a distinct outlook on life. They do not allow their emotions to affect their judgments or ignore certain character defects in a woman when in a relationship.

This section will discuss warning signs that sigma males never miss in a woman. Once a sigma male identifies certain characteristics, he quickly loses interest in a woman, regardless of how attractive, intellectual, or impressive she may appear. Regardless of how much a sigma male loves a woman, the red flags highlighted in this book will convince him to alter his mind.

Without further ado, here are the red flags that sigma males never miss in a female.

Women Who Are Broke, Dependent, and Feel Entitled

Sigma males cannot tolerate needy and financially dependent women who feel entitled. The lone wolves are aware that these ladies are a permanent burden, and they will deplete you both psychologically and financially. Sigma males consider most energy draining women to be a distraction. Therefore, she must acquire a job and gain independence before being ready for a relationship. And for the entitled, she assume you are inherently responsible for her costs because you are in a relationship.

Once a sigma male recognizes this feature in a woman, he terminates the relationship. Do not misunderstand; sigma males do not dislike caring for their females. But overly-dependent and uneducated women are nuisances, and they are never content and rarely grateful for your efforts on their behalf anyway. Therefore, the sigma male would prefer to remain single than be with a needy, dependent, and entitled woman.

Women With a Male Best Friend

Sigma males frown at their lady having a close male buddy, and this connection cannot exist. Don't get me wrong. The sigma males lack insecurity and have sufficient knowledge of humanity to see that most of these male "best friends" always have hidden objectives. 'Male best friends' are the guardians of these women's emotional trash more often than not. They reveal everything to their best friend, even their relationship status. Sigma males enjoy maintaining their privacy, and they desire that everything that occurs within the relationship remains within the relationship. To a sigma male, a woman who has a male best friend cannot be wholly devoted to the relationship.

To begin with, male closest friends frequently conceal affections for women. Moreover, throughout the process of issue sharing, various emotions are exchanged. When a male "best friend" offers a woman a shoulder to lean on, he may provide her with a "dick to ride on."

In addition, a male best friend's presence generates unneeded rivalry, something a sigma male cannot accomplish. If you know lone wolves well, you will learn they do not desire to impress others. According to a study, a woman is more likely to develop romantic feelings for her male best friend since she only perceives his positive attributes. Sigma males dislike rivalry in relationships, and if you spend too much time with a male best friend, he will quit the relationship without debate.

Unintelligence

Sigma males are clever, intellectual, and wise. And they always want to be with an intellectual and savvy lady and someone with whom they may engage in intellectually fascinating discourse. This may surprise you, but sigma males cannot stand stupid women. To date a sigma male, you must have made personal investments. A high-value guy, such as the sigma male, will pursue a woman with high worth. He cannot accept mediocrity, and you must give something of value. If not, you are unsuitable for the sigma male.

Poor Communication

Sigma males cannot date women with poor communication skills, and every connection depends on effective communication. Therefore, a woman cannot vibe well with a sigma male if she cannot have a decent dialogue with her or express her emotions.

She Has a Low Self Esteem

Low self-esteem in women is troublesome, and Sigma males cannot deal with them because they are perpetually insecure, envious, and constantly seeking attention and approval. When a sigma male discovers his partner has poor self-esteem, he instantly stops the relationship.

What Happens If a Sigma Male Ignores a Woman

Regarding relationships, sigma males can be perceived as "weirdos." Despite their oddness, women find them appealing. Sigma males comprehend the psychology of women superbly. Sigma males cherish, adore, and facilitate the lives of cooperative and understanding women. But as soon as a woman gives the lone wolf trouble and attempts to make his life unpleasant, he promptly disregards her. It makes no difference if he is married or dating that woman. Once a woman attempts to make the sigma male's life miserable, he will disregard her permanently. There will always be instances when a woman attempts to perform a trick or behave when she expects her guy to respond. Beta, omega, and even alpha men will always respond emotionally or seem dissatisfied and disturbed in such a circumstance. Such responses will give the lady the feeling that she has triumphed. And you will be playing on her field.

Do not misunderstand; sigma males cherish, adore, and facilitate the lives of cooperative and understanding women. But as soon as a woman gives the lone wolf trouble and attempts to make his life unpleasant, he promptly disregards her. It makes no difference if he is married or dating that woman. Once a woman attempts to make the sigma male's life miserable, he will disregard her permanently. There will always be instances when a woman attempts to perform a trick or behave when she expects her guy to respond. Beta, omega, and even alpha men will always respond emotionally or seem dissatisfied and disturbed in such a circumstance. Such responses will give the lady the feeling that she has triumphed. And you will be playing on her field.

However, sigma males never react emotionally towards females, and the lone wolf will maintain his stoicism regardless of what the woman does. When it becomes essential to take action, sigma males will guarantee that they have emotional control. Once the sigma male no longer reacts to women's games, he will grow dissatisfied because he realizes it is impossible to govern lone wolves. Therefore, in a relationship, sigma males consistently disregard what women do, which will convince the female that she cannot play, manipulate, or run with the sigma males.

Women usually acquiesce and collaborate with lone wolves because sigma males do not always give in to women's demands or mental gymnastics or allow them enough time to dwell on their negative concerns. Once a woman discovers that her guy is emotional and constantly enables her actions to define how he feels, acts, and even thinks, she will control and dominate him in the relationship. Sigma males comprehend the psychological tricks women constantly engage in, and they never fall for them. Observing a typical Beta or Omega male relationship reveals that these men are perpetually confused with their partners. And they are constantly curious as to why their wives behave a certain way. Unfortunately, this fascination with female behavior makes it simple for women to captivate Beta, omega, and occasionally alpha guys.

Sigma males are exceptional in analyzing women's behavior, and they know that not every woman's conduct merits a response. Because some women may not have a happy and enjoyable life, they prefer to surround themselves with tension and problems. And if you don't figure this out before it's too late, it will do you more harm than good. Therefore, anytime a sigma male interacts with a woman, he employs patience and the skill of ignoring women. To a sigma male, women are like one's shadow; the more one moves away from them, the closer they follow. However, when you approach them, they retreat.

When you neglect a lady, you create a mystery in her mind about what you're doing. Even if a sigma male loves a woman so much, he never demonstrates it to the point where she feels she can control his day or actions. Sigma males know that the most effective method for gaining a woman's cooperation is not to respond emotionally. However, ignoring them creates the idea that you don't care about their actions.

It's awful that some men still pay for what harm previous men may have caused to their wives even if it was years ago. Therefore, sigma males will always disregard a woman when she raises an issue that does not directly concern them. Whether it's an ex-girlfriend or a woman he wants, ignoring is the most effective approach for sigma males to grab a woman's attention. When a sigma male disregards a woman, she loses her head and wonders, "Doesn't he care about me?" Am I insufficient for him? Or, perhaps I could clean up my behavior so that he will be interested in me. Because sigma males have learned to ignore the needy attention of some women through time, they wouldn't lose sleep over such women. They need to ignore them and act as if they never existed. This will alter the woman's current beliefs and change her perspective. Before gaining the sigma male's attention, a woman must show her value. Otherwise, she will be treated like any other woman would be. This explains why some women place some men (perhaps Beta and omega) in the friend zone and refer to them as "Nice Guys" while yearning to sleep with a man they have just met.

Unique Ways Sigma Males Show Their Love

Sigma males are more desirable to women as they look more enigmatic and elusive. However, it may be pretty challenging to determine how sigma males express their affection. This section will describe the ways sigma males express their affection.

They Will Express Their Interest to You

In general, sigma males do not talk excessively about themselves. The closer you get to him, the more enigmatic he becomes. But if the sigma males love someone, they will begin to relax around them. Once a sigma male begins to share intimate secrets about his life with you, it is evident that he loves and cares for you. To a sigma male, it is more romantic than a movie date or romantic supper to learn more about the person they love. The lone wolf dislikes the display of affection in public, and they would prefer to express their love in a private setting.

They will Reveal Their Vulnerabilities

Sigma males have little confidence in others. Whenever lone wolves interact with others, they anticipate the worst and hope for the best. They are more intellectual than emotional while in a relationship. However, if a sigma male feels comfortable around someone, he reveals his vulnerability to that person. Remember that sigma males are indifferent to what others think of them. He won't mind revealing his weaknesses when he finds his perfect lady since he will be at ease with her.

They View You as Their go-to Resource

Typically, sigma males enjoy being alone, and they attempt to tackle it independently regardless of the circumstance. However, once they fall in love with someone, they progressively share the ups and downs of their lives with them. So, sigma males demonstrate affection by relying on you for most tasks. They will confide in you whenever anything brings them joy or sorrow. They will feel comfortable sharing their emotions and frustrations with you because they have faith in you and believe you can relate to them. They Display Their Romantic Sides Oh! Wait! What were you contemplating? Do you find sigma males to be uninteresting? That is not the case. Sigma males are rather romantic, but it takes them some time to reveal their passionate side. Nevertheless, if a sigma male reveals his romantic side, it is evident that he loves you.

Sigma males express romance most remarkably. They may go trekking with you, take a road trip, engage in stimulating and thought-provoking conversations, etc. Once a sigma male is sure that you are the one, they will demonstrate the essence of romance. Therefore, women who date sigma males consider them invaluable. The affection you will receive from sigma males cannot be found anywhere.

You Will Become an Integral Part of Their Daily Routine

Sigma males prefer to spend time alone, which is the only way to replenish their creative energy and contemplate the world around them. However, when a sigma male discovers the ideal lady who understands him and views the world through his eyes, he makes time to speak with her. Whether or not the sigma male is busy, he will include that person into his everyday routine if he loves someone.

Things Sigma Males Never Say to a Woman

Sigma Males have a profound understanding of the psychology behind women's behaviors. They are aware of women's mental games and employ a paradoxical strategy to counteract these games.

This section will cover the things males should never say to women.

Ask a Woman to be Their Girlfriend

This may sound strange, but sigma males never ask a woman to become their girlfriend. Instead, lone wolves will present themselves in a manner that makes women desire to be with them. Sigma males know that once they commit to a woman, she may take advantage of this since she no longer sees them as challenging. I mean that women quickly lose interest in a man who gives up his commitment readily.

Women seek to encourage you to pursue a relationship with them rather than initiating contact. Sigma males are aware of this psychological phenomenon, so they never ask a woman to be their girlfriend.

Ask Women What They Should Do

Despite how odd it may appear, women like macho males and desire a man who can steer and guide them. Women like being invited along for the adventure and ride, and they dislike situations in which they must make a choice. Sigma males are aware of this truth. So, instead of the sigma male asking his partner, "Where do you want to spend the weekend?" or, "What do you want to do?" Instead, he would say, "I have plans for us this weekend, so please come over."

Discuss Their Shortcomings or Life Difficulties with Women

Wait!!! Men open out to women about their flaws and difficulties in life? Oops!!! That is likely something that Beta and Omega males will do. Not the sigma males, however. The lone wolves always keep their cards close to their chests. Typically, sigma males conceal their faults and difficulties. Ladies will pretend to comprehend your situation and even attempt to soothe you, but people already have a distinct opinion of you and will begin to view you differently. Women value guys who solve issues rather than those who whine about them.

Inquire Whether a Woman Has a Boyfriend

When a sigma male encounters a woman, he automatically believes she is single, and he will accept whatever comes his way and keep things going with her. Asking a lady whether she has a partner communicates a lack of self-confidence.

Request a Woman's Phone Number

Sigma males interact with women similarly to how salespeople interact with clients. They never ask for a woman's number; instead, they provide their number for the woman to call. Once the lone wolf offers a lady his phone number, she has the idea that he is not desperate and in need.

Express Their Feelings to a Newly Met Woman

No matter how deeply a sigma male loves a woman, he never expresses his affection for her. Sigma males have emotional control and maintain composure until the lady they are interested in expresses her feelings. Once you express your feelings for a lady, she will become bored with you. Women adore intriguing males who keep them on their toes. They will hang out with a lady and enjoy themselves together, but they will never be romantic.

How Sigma Males Get Dates With Most Single Women

Sigma males have a very different view of women, and he respects them, but he feels that every woman is single. Whether she has a partner or is engaged, sigma males will always assume she is single. In reality, sigma males have seen men whose girlfriend or wife slept with a number of men. The partners of these women went above and above to provide them with a comfortable life. However, they continue to cheat at every chance. Some men sacrifice their goals and work jobs they dislike to provide their wives with a comfortable lifestyle. However, guess what? These ladies will continue to deceive them at every chance. You now see why you cannot blame the sigma male for assuming that all women are single.

Most guys (most likely Beta and Omega males) feel that if they have incredible sex with a woman, she will never leave them. They assume the lady is immediately theirs if she yells their name or calls them daddy during intercourse. However, some men are unmoved by these signals and bedroom antics. This is because they recognize that women are masters of deceit. And women now are far more promiscuous than in the past. It is simple for women to date any man with dating apps and other media platforms. The lone wolves know that modern women seek enjoyment and are less concerned about commitment.

Once a man has spoken the proper thing to a lady and given her butterflies, he may have a sexual relationship with her. As a result of this unpleasant reality, many guys feel that every woman is single. Women are constantly present-minded and just devoted to the man who will provide them with the greatest stimulation. In reality, your girlfriend belongs to her feelings, not to you. Sigma males are aware that no one ever possesses a woman because women are continually searching for a new sparkling toy. There are occasions when some women could be holding hands with their boyfriends but continue to gaze at the sigma male. She may even offer the lone wolf her phone number discreetly. However, you know that sigma males do not call, and they would provide the woman with their phone number so she may contact them. No matter how much you believe your girlfriend loves you, it's often said she may leave you if she meets the right man. I refer to the man she finds handsome and who sweeps her off her feet.

Most of the time, when a woman hangs out or goes on a road trip with her best friend, she is not simply out for fun. She seeks the next person who can provide her with the enjoyment she desires. She has already committed to a lasting relationship with you and is now seeking the enjoyable moments in between.

Sigma males recognize that women do not wear cosmetics, eyelashes, and tight clothing for enjoyment. The fact is that she is seeking a new relationship, a new man. In reality, nothing can truly please a woman over the long run, and she is perpetually sad and desires new experiences.

The truth is that women experience greater satisfaction when they participate in various interactions with multiple guys. Sigma males view most women as opportunists, and they spend their time snapping photos on Instagram and Facebook to attract attention and perhaps a handsome man.

Sigma males feel that a woman's only loyalty is to her goal. And what is the goal of a woman? A woman's goal is to absorb, extract, and discover the ideal male to fulfill her desires. That is a financially secure way of living. Therefore, she will constantly seek the best bargain and dump you as soon as the opportunity arises. Hey! It is simply a part of who they are, inherent to their biology. At all times, a woman's desires and demands take precedence. She will leave you without remorse once she determines that another guy can give her superior closeness and a more comfortable lifestyle.

Sigma males feel that a woman's only loyalty is to her goal. And what is the goal of a woman? A woman's goal is to absorb, extract, and discover the ideal male to fulfill her desires. Sigma males are sure that you will never be the sole man in her life, and she will always have many men on standby. And as soon as things become a little tense between you two, she is already planning her next move. Each woman requires security, enjoyment, and adventure, and they find it difficult to depend on one man regardless of the circumstances.

Reasons Sigma Males Never Chase Women

Sigma males are incredibly intent. They always place their life goals above everything else, and they base their entire lives on their objectives. This explains why others view them as elusive and mysterious. However, these two characteristics are why lone wolves are distinctive and typically more successful than their peers.

This section will talk about why sigma males never chase women. Every sigma male believes that chasing women is a bad idea. And that is because they consider it the greatest thing that can distract them from achieving their life goals and purpose. Sigma males believe that if a woman loves and wants to be in a relationship, she won't make them do the chasing. But most times, a woman will make a man chase her if she doesn't like that man. These women enjoy the thrill of being chased, giving them a sense of value and importance. Sigma males don't waste their time chasing women. They can easily tell if a woman is in love with them from how she talks, her availability, her body language, and how free she is whenever she is around them.

So, here are three reasons why sigma males never chase women;

It Distracts Them from Focusing on the Important Things

Sigma males have great goals and aspirations and are always preoccupied with achieving their goals and making their dreams a reality. You see, chasing women is not part of their priority at all. Sigma males can never waste their precious time chasing women instead of their dreams. They believe that time is a precious resource, and every second you spend not chasing your dreams and aspirations is lost forever. So, they are always laser-focused on their dreams and goals. And once they are successful, women will chase them.

It makes a Man Seems Desperate and Pathetic Before a Lady

When a man chases a woman, she usually feels the man is bugging them. And this happens when the feeling is not mutual, and the love is unrequited. Even if a sigma male asks a woman out, once she says no, he will move on immediately. You will never see a sigma male bugging a woman. They believe that if you put in so much effort just to get a lady's attention, it feels like you are coercing her into a relationship with you. It's a complete waste of time and energy to keep pursuing a lady after making it clear to you that she is not interested. And you will come across as desperate and pathetic when you keep chasing women.

Key Takeaways

- Women test a sigma male to determine his strength, and having well-developed muscles does not indicate strength.

- Most women desire a man with a masculine appearance. But ladies like to be with a man with mental and emotional power and physical strength. When a woman evaluates a sigma male, she evaluates his emotional strength.

- The more semen the sigma males retain, the more energy, confidence, and masculinity they will develop.

- Women usually acquiesce and collaborate with lone wolves because sigma males do not always give in to women's demands or mental gymnastics or allow them enough time to dwell on their negative concerns.

- Sigma males do not talk excessively about themselves. The closer you get to him, the more enigmatic he becomes. But if the sigma males love someone, they will begin to relax around them.

- Sigma males have ambitious goals and aspirations and are always preoccupied with achieving their goals and making their dreams a reality. And chasing women is not part of their priority at all. Sigma males can never waste their precious time chasing women instead of their dreams.

CONCLUSION

A sigma male is an introverted guy who is self-assured. He prefers to exist outside the alpha, delta, and beta personalities. He is not scared to be unique or to stand out in a crowd. He is self-assured in his style and understands what he wants out of life. He does not need the affirmation or approval of others. Sigma males are sometimes perceived as distant or withdrawn. However, they are just introverts who enjoy a peaceful existence away from the limelight.

This is the epitome of a sigma male. These guys, unlike alpha males, are more reserved and will listen before speaking. They are excellent listeners and only speak after considerable thinking when they are among others. They do not seek approval from others, but if they do, they will not go out of their way to acquire it again. They are incredibly self-sufficient and do not require any form of recognition from others to feel happy about themselves.

Some individuals mistakenly feel that to lead, you must wield power. However, this is not actually the case. In reality, the style of a sigma male leader is to lead by example or mutual agreement. Sigma male leaders will accomplish more by taking a more balanced attitude to others, knowing and respecting people more. They are also interested in their followers' life, preparing them for the future.

The male sigma is also a fantastic personality in relationships and society. The sigma male demonstrates good conduct and behaviors - this often does not imply commonly recognized behavioral standards in today's society. Cheating and bad habits are not evidence of a true man but rather his frailty. A sigma man must battle both himself and his flaws. He must continuously demonstrate determination and do something. He can assist others, which is significant and vital. In a relationship, this is what a sigma guy should be.

A sigma male recognizes that a woman is always emotionally and psychologically stronger than a male. Only a guy with a strong intellect and grasp of interpersonal psychology can realistically understand the nature of women. To do this, a sigma male must grow as a person and commit significant time to self-education and the study of several problems.

Above all, sigma males are passionate guys who love their jobs and actively want to accomplish professional outcomes; who like their girlfriends, and constantly want to do something good for themselves and the environment they find themselves in.

Dear Reader,

As independent authors it's often difficult to gather reviews compared with much bigger publishers.

Therefore, please leave a review on the platform where you bought this book.

Many thanks,

Author Team

Want Free New Book Launches?
Email us at:
mindsetmastership@gmail.com

Printed in Great Britain
by Amazon